THE PROFIT ADVISOR

THE NEW ROLE OF ACCOUNTANTS AND BOOKKEEPERS

FEMKE HOGEMA

ISBN: 9789493056404 (ebook)

ISBN: 9789493056398 (paperback)

Publisher: Amsterdam Publishers

info@amsterdampublishers.com

Copyright © 2020 Femke Hogema

Translation: Ron Rosenbrand, Betterwords

Proofreader: Meggan Robinson

Original: *De Winstadviseur*, 2018, Van Duuren Management

All right reserved. No part of this book may be used or reproduced by any means, graphic, electronical or mechanical, including photocopying, recording, taping, or by any information storage retrieval system without the written permission of the publisher except in the case of brief quotations embodied in critical articles and reviews.

TESTIMONIALS

Understanding the value you can provide for your clients once you move past your traditional role and into the advisory role is hard to imagine unless you've done it - until now. Femke walks you through the process in a way that's clear, easy to follow and realistic. The needs of the entrepreneur are changing and if you're not positioned to partner with your clients as their trusted and much needed advisor, you're falling behind. I would urge you to read and implement everything she teaches in this book now! - **Lisa Campbell, CPB, CPFP, Profit Strategist, The Marcam Group, Canada**

I'm a raving superfan. This book is a MUST for all financial advisors, especially tax experts, who crave to become a trusted advisor for their customers. Embrace the opportunities, that come with the development of artificial intelligence - start your journey now and help your customers to grow a healthy, thriving and profitable business. It's all laid out in this book - step by step!
- **Benita Königbauer, Steuerberaterin, Germany**

In *The Profit Advisor* Femke builds four foundational pillars for the future of the accounting profession. Accounts production is the beginning of the conversation with the client, not the end. To be an outstanding advisor, you have to be emotionally and proactively invested in your client's goals. The client's understanding of how you can help them beyond the basics cannot be assumed, they need to be educated on an ongoing basis.

For an advisor to reach their own goals, they must be intentional and specific in their planning. This is the first time I have read a book which brings together all the aspects required for a 21st century accounting professional to thrive rather than survive, as standard.

Most importantly, the book challenges the reader to act and then provides a framework for doing exactly that, which is critical for any professional looking to escape 'The Compliance Trap'. - **Martin Bissett, Founder - The Upward Spiral Partnership Ltd, United Kingdom**

The Profit Advisor clearly explains the challenge that both business owners and their accountants face in working together. Technology is changing rapidly and constantly. Business is moving faster than ever. Accountants must move quickly too to provide their clients with relevant information to guide them towards profitability. Having been on this journey myself with my accounting practice, this book helped me refine my product offerings to ensure we are meeting our clients' needs and are helping them to achieve their profit goals. This book is easy to read and will give you the steps necessary to move you down the advisory path quickly. - **Cyndi Thomason, CEO/Founder bookskeep, USA**

Femke Hogema describes a new role for bookkeepers and accountants. Taking up this new role is important as change is a constant in our industry. Hogema explains that digitalization can help entrepreneurs to make better business choices, and at the same time gives accountants a world of opportunities. The Profit Advisor can help financials take the next step in their career, as accountant, bookkeeper, or: Profit advisor. Because with a new role comes a new title. - **André Kwakernaat, founder Twinfield and Director Business Innovations Wolters Kluwer Tax & Accounting Europe**

Femke puts her finger on the sore spot in the accounting industry. But she does more: she also offers concrete solutions. She describes in clear words what the challenges are and where opportunities lie. This book gives answers to questions companies have and it is filled with practical tools for financial advisors who want to give more added value to clients. A must read for all in the finance industry. - **Michel Hamer, director NOAB (Dutch Organization for Bookkeepers and Tax Advisors)**

The Profit Advisor is a must-read for accountants and CPAs, committed to serving the needs of their entrepreneurial clients. As a Business Psychologist, I work with entrepreneurs daily who are eager for better guidance from their accountants. Pro-active planning and strategy, based on solid financials, are missing in too many small businesses, and it's a setup for the owner to toil away for years, never realizing the full profit potential in the business. You are well-positioned to change that. Within *The Profit Advisor* you will find solid guidance and tools to support you in expanding your impact. - **Sabrina Starling, PhD, Author,** *How to Hire the Best***, Tap the Potential LLC, USA**

The Profit Advisor is a practical guide for bookkeepers, CPAs, and accountants looking for a way to increase the value of the services they provide to their clients. Many people in the accounting and bookkeeping industry get caught up in doing compliance work like bookkeeping, payroll and tax preparation. We are quickly coming to the day when computer learning, advanced software, and artificial intelligence replace many in the accounting and bookkeeping industry.

If you want to become more valuable to your clients, *The Profit Advisor* is a must-read for you. Femke, in her no-nonsense book, The Profit Advisor, gives you a complete, step by step framework you need to give your clients what they desperately need, but can't seem to find. You must read it!!

Here's the best part. By applying Femke's words in the Profit Advisor, you'll earn more money, you'll have better clients, you'll do work that transforms businesses, and provide you with a level of fulfillment you didn't know was possible. - **Damon Yudichak, CPA, MBA, PFP, USA**

CONTENTS

Foreword by Mike Michalowicz	ix
Foreword	xi
Introduction	xiii
Reader's guide	xix
1. New opportunities for the accounting profession	1
2. Your mission and vision	19
3. Deliver results, not actions	31
4. Administration in 30 minutes per week plus one minute per day	61
5. Support your client in making a Profitable Plan	82
6. Managing with Profit First	97
7. Selling high-priced advisory services	115
8. Create an unrivalled client experience	146
9. Powerful client communication	164
10. Communication skills for specific challenges	192
11. Your company as a well-oiled machine	207
Conclusion and implementation plan	239
Bibliography	241
About the Author	243
Acknowledgments	245

FOREWORD BY MIKE MICHALOWICZ

"We need this!"

Those were the first words Femke Hogema said when we met. She and her husband Bart had made the long trip to visit the Profit First Professionals offices in New Jersey. Femke had discovered my book Profit First, heard about our process of certifying accountants and bookkeepers in this process, and realized this was an opportunity for accountants and bookkeepers in The Netherlands.

That was nearly five years ago, and today I am proud to say Femke is a close friend. She is the authority in The Netherlands on profit strategies and as a result is redefining the accounting industry. She is positioning accountants, bookkeepers and financial professionals to be consultants to their clients again. No longer relegated to plugging in data, producing reports and managing tax compliance, Femke is making accounting professionals a vital resource for entrepreneurs.

How? She realized that accounting professionals need to provide consulting services around profit and profit strategies. I am proud to say that Femke has mastered the Profit First process and translated it into Dutch. She is the founder of Profit First Professionals in The Netherlands, growing to more than 75 active accounting professionals. And, perhaps most importantly, has gone on to be the most recognized authority on money management in The Netherlands. She has written game changing books for accounting professionals and even hosted a popular television show helping entrepreneurs achieve profitability.

The face of accounting is undergoing its biggest change in over 300 years. With the advent of advanced technologies, the computers can do (or soon will be doing) the data management, the production of reports and tax compliance. Accounting professionals need to transition to consulting work or become irrelevant.

If you are an accounting professional, what you hold in your hands with this book is the most important information you can have. This book is not stuck in theory and noble ideas... instead it walks you through the exact steps you need to be successful. You will discover how to serve your clients in a new way, exactly the way they want and need you to serve them. And – this won't be a surprise – you will discover how to help your clients with their (and your) number one need... profit.

Turn off the distractions, grab your favorite beverage, and dig deep into this book. It will be time well spent. And when you are finished reading the book, I think you will be as grateful to know Femke as I am. She is that good. This book is that good. Enjoy.

Mike Michalowicz, author of Profit First

FOREWORD

The world of accounting is changing dramatically, and that's no surprise. That you, as a CPA, accountant, bookkeeper or financial specialist, must start offering other services is also no surprise.

The big questions are: What services should you offer? And how do you go about repositioning yourself and your company?

This book provides practical answers to these pressing questions. For more than ten years, I have been providing financial expertise to freelancers and SMEs, even though I don't actually do their bookkeeping. My clients needed financial advice in addition to the work their accountant does, and I have developed and refined methods, techniques and products that have helped tens of thousands of entrepreneurs build financially healthy and profitable businesses.

I have finally written the book that has been in my head for five years: a book with which I give you, a financial expert with self-employed and SME clients, the valuable tools to help your clients build financially healthy and profitable companies.

Dozens of accountants, bookkeepers and CPAs have read this book before it went to the printer. They said things like:

"Femke hits the nail on the head with *The Profit Advisor!*"

"This book provides an answer to the 'how' question."

"It gives me very concrete tools to get to work."

"It is a valuable reference work that contains so much that it will serve me for a long time."

"The information (from ICT to communication and from pricing to sales) is expertly presented and easy to read."

In this book, I transfer my knowledge, vision and skills to you as a financial expert. My goal is twofold: I wish for you, as a profit advisor, to run a sustainable business, generate more profit and enjoy your work more. And I wish for all entrepreneurs to find and work with profit advisors who help them build financially healthy and profitable businesses!

Femke Hogema

INTRODUCTION

Developers of smart software, progressive accounting firms and even tax authorities are doing their utmost to ensure that accounting and tax preparation require less and less specialized knowledge. In fact, some experts believe that in several years the accounting profession will no longer exist. Oxford economists Carl Frey and Michael Osborne researched the probability of computerization for 702 detailed occupations.[1] The occupation in place 1 is the least susceptible to computerization, while the occupation in place 702 is most susceptible to computerization. Accountants and auditors are in place 589, bookkeeping, accounting, and auditing clerks in place 671, and tax preparers in place 695.

That's bleak news for people who work in these vulnerable fields.

But is this really a doomsday scenario? Or do technological developments create a sea of opportunities and make the profession of financial expert more interesting and attractive? I think the latter. But it won't happen by itself. You will have to take action to make it happen.

It starts with abandoning the idea that your profession is mainly about registering and reporting facts. That is something that computers will soon do (or already do) better than people. In fact, Dutch accounting firm 216 has been offering its clients free standard services, such as preparing annual accounts, since 2017. How does 216 stay in business if they're giving away accounting services? They bill their clients for the valuable financial advice they provide.[2]

As accounting automation increases, entrepreneurs frequently transition to handling their books themselves. Online accounting software is becoming more and more intuitive and is increasingly geared to the knowledge and needs of entrepreneurs who don't have any accounting knowledge. Online accounting software systems like Quickbooks and Xero are increasing in popularity. As even the tax collection departments (IRS, HMRC and others) are becoming savvier to new technology, accounting professionals need to develop new skills and services or they will miss the innovation boat.

We always thought that accounting was the goal, but what if accounting is no longer the goal but rather the foundation? What if records are in order and tax returns and annual accounts are delivered without you or your client having to invest much time, energy, or money in generating them? What will your profession look like then?

If you as a financial expert want to be of value to your clients, you will need to help them use their numbers. You will need to help them manage money, plan for profits and make financially sound choices. Your role will be helping your clients build financially healthy and profitable businesses. In other words, you must become a profit advisor.

You may be wondering if there is any demand for profit advisors, but the proof of such demand has been evident for years. Money, finances, making a profit... these are often difficult subjects for entrepreneurs (for people in general, actually). In fact, when people who are self-employed or own SMEs are asked about the biggest bottleneck in their business, effective accounting is one of the first challenges mentioned.[3]

Entrepreneurs often have so much difficulty with the financial side of their business that they go into denial about its importance. "I have an accountant for that," they say. They bury their heads in the sand and use you, their accountant, as an alibi. Or they claim that money is not important, because that's not what life is all about. They say, for example: "As long as I do what I am good at, the money will follow naturally." They absolve themselves of the responsibility of running a financially healthy and profitable business. They need a profit advisor to help them get this essential aspect of their business in order.

A business is a wonderful vehicle for entrepreneurs to make their dreams and goals – whatever they may be – come true. But too often it doesn't work. Entrepreneurs often have big dreams: to help people, to save the world, to innovate, but they can't translate those dreams to a profitable reality. They can't actually get their businesses off the ground. They tinker with their margins. They don't make enough money, have financial worries, cannot invest, and fail to make their desired impact. The lack of financial insight causes enormous suffering among entrepreneurs. Too often, that suffering is concealed.

This can and must change. Thanks to technological developments, accounting has become a commodity whose value is decreasing. It's an activity in which we no longer need to invest much time, money or energy. The good news for entrepreneurs is that this time, money and energy can be freed up for something more important: building financially healthy businesses. As an accountant, a financial expert, you are positioned to capitalize on this opportunity and provide a valuable service. Your clients trust you. You know their numbers. You know the tricky matters in their finances. Your clients are waiting for you to become their profit advisor.

Your new role requires you to help your clients determine their financial goals and to chart a course toward success. It requires you to be a coach and accountability partner. You, too, must commit to client goals and reframe your mindset to sell results instead of actions.

Your new role as a profit advisor will require new skills, such as coaching and sales. Simply being a numbers whiz won't be enough anymore. You'll need to acquire new knowledge about systems and methods to guide entrepreneurs toward a profitable business. Perhaps it even requires a different mindset, about what kind of client you want or do not want, on which basis you are paid and how far your responsibility extends in supporting your client.

This book provides you with concrete tools, methods and information to become a profit advisor and will help you achieve the following results:

1. You will not lose your clients in the current, rapidly developing financial market. Even better, you will acquire clients who have walked away from bookkeepers and accountants who aren't able to deliver enough value.

2. You will offer value that goes far beyond just putting accounts

in order. You will help your clients build financially healthy and profitable businesses.

3. You will get more satisfaction from your work, because you will be helping clients achieve meaningful results.

4. You will earn more with less effort. You will say goodbye to hourly billing and start earning in line with the value you add.

5. You, as an entrepreneur, will run a company that offers that value to your clients in a consistent way.

---

1. https://www.oxfordmartin.ox.ac.uk/downloads/academic/The_Future_of_Employment.pdf
2. See www.216.nl
3. Research by the independent market and policy research bureau Panteia shows that 52% of the SME entrepreneurs find the administration the biggest bottleneck in their business operations.

READER'S GUIDE

Chapter 1 lays out the developments in the accounting profession, and Chapter 2 covers the significance of these developments for your role, vision and mission. Chapter 3 discusses what your clients really need and how you can deliver it. Chapters 4, 5 and 6 will teach you practical methods you can use to help your clients actually make a better profit. Chapter 7 is about selling valuable and higher-priced services to your clients. Chapter 8 explains how to ensure your clients have unparalleled client experiences. Chapters 9 and 10 offer you the communication skills and coaching techniques to attract, support, and retain your clients. Chapter 11 is about your company and how you can run it in such a way that it delivers results even when you don't put in any hours yourself. To make this book complete, I offer you an implementation plan.

At the end of each chapter you'll find an action step. Take this step. Just reading this book will do little or nothing to boost your success. Knowledge is only of value when it is converted into action.

For the sake of readability, I sometimes refer to accountants, sometimes to bookkeepers or CPAs and often to financial specialists, financial experts, financial and profit advisors, and by that I always mean anyone who recognizes himself in the context of this book.

I have worked with many entrepreneurs and often their accountant, bookkeeper or CPA was involved in the process. The cumulative experiences of my clients and their accountants have formed the basis for the story about entrepreneur Peter and his accountant Greg. At the beginning of each chapter you can read about the process that both Peter and Greg are going through. Peter and Greg are not based on one individual entrepreneur and his accountant, but are composites based on many entrepreneurs and accountants who have faced very real challenges.

1 NEW OPPORTUNITIES FOR THE ACCOUNTING PROFESSION

* * *

Denying technological developments just isn't that clever - Martijn Aslander

* * *

This is how Peter and Greg's story begins

Peter designs apps, and he is pretty good at it. You can share your ideas and he will make it happen. And not just for you – he works mainly for large international companies. Quite a cool guy, I thought. He contacted me because, as he explained, he "was not a numbers person." With an annual revenue of over 300,000 dollars and growing, he felt he needed to get a better grip on his finances. He was not making enough profit and was feeling increasingly uneasy about the financial side of his business. I was going to help Peter create a financially healthy and profitable company.

To better understand Peter's company, I paid him a visit. He had a huge garage next to his office. The garage housed, in addition to large servers, two Volkswagen vans. "Beautiful," I said.

Peter immediately began to talk enthusiastically about them. They were his pride and passion. He enjoyed tinkering with them. "But," he said with a sad face, "I don't have time for them anymore. I work fourteen hours a day." I could feel his pain. And my motivation increased to help Peter come to grips with his finances.

We walked into his office, where he explained to me how he managed his accounts. His story was not unique. Bookkeeping used up a lot of his energy. At the end of each quarter, he would search every nook and cranny in his office for receipts, so that he could file his VAT return. He checked his bank balance daily and when he noticed he had been paid, he would breathe a sigh of relief, because that meant he could pay the bills.

There was a lot of room for efficiency improvements. For example, the absence of proper processes cost both him and his accountant a lot of time and hard-earned cash, but his lack of insight presented an even bigger problem. When I asked him about his margin on the apps, he didn't have an answer. He frequently hired whiz kids to help him develop the software, and his investments in IT were also considerable, but he had no idea how much profit he was making. His accountant's reports didn't help him either. The last annual financial statements were from more than two years before we met! Not being an archaeologist, I wasn't really interested in those.

"But he's a good accountant, mind you," Peter said. "And not cheap either. I pay him more than 7,000 dollars a year." Yes, seriously... 7,000 dollars for digging up dinosaurs. And the situation only got worse as I continued to dig.

"What is your salary?" I asked to get an idea of how much one can actually earn building apps.

"None," he said. "We live on my wife's salary. I invest everything back in my company."

I know that "investing" is often a euphemism for "costs, costs and more costs," so I started to worry even more. Here was a man with a passion, the best app builder in the country. He knew how to find clients and how to sell. After all, a revenue of 300K doesn't come out of thin air. At the same time, he had no idea where he stood, where he wanted to go or how to get there. His accountant didn't help him either, because he was two years behind. The combination of an old-fashioned accountant and the lack of the right processes cost him a lot of money. He had no time for his hobby and his wife had to earn for both of them.

But there was something even more worrying. Peter wasn't aware of the fact that he was running a financially unhealthy business. He thought things were going well (because the revenue was high) and that he was being smart (because he "invested" everything back into his company). But a company that doesn't make a profit is not a healthy company. A company that doesn't take care of you is not a strong company. Peter wasn't building anything; he was creating a cash-eating monster. Worst of all, he was completely unaware of the gravity of the situation. He had been operating this way for five years. He had a good reputation. He was the best in the country. He didn't realize that he had not built anything. When he went on holiday, business would grind to a halt. Without Peter, there was no business. And with Peter, there wasn't really a business either.

As a last attempt to make Peter understand the seriousness of the matter I said, "Peter, if you had taken a paper route five years ago instead of starting this company, you would have more money now and you could have worked on your VW vans for twelve hours a day." I saw this startled him, but I could tell it was shock mingled with disbelief.

We made a follow-up appointment with his accountant. To understand where we should be heading, I first had to know where we stood.

* * *

This chapter gives a broad overview of the developments in the accounting profession, the real needs of the entrepreneur and the new role of the financial professional.

In the first section, I challenge you to no longer see accounting as your primary objective, but as the indispensable foundation on which you build your reputation as a profit advisor. I then shift the focus to entrepreneurs themselves; why do they need a profit advisor? The third section discusses the innovations that underlie our pressing need to re-envision the accounting profession. The last section of this chapter deals with the significance of these innovations for your sector.

1.1 Accounting is not the goal; it is the foundation

The accountant's objective has always been to do the books, draw up the annual reports and file the tax returns. Of course, giving advice is not new to accountants, but that was usually an additional service. Accounting was the primary objective. Ask yourself these questions: "What if accounting is not the goal? What does my profession look like then?" What if accounting is like the foundation of a new house to be built? Without the foundation there is no house – at least, not a sustainable one. But, at the same time, the builder's client never thinks about the foundation. The client envisions the new modern kitchen, or the

French doors to the garden, or the solid wood floor that gives a warm glow to the house. Those are the clients' goals. That's what they dream of. The contractor understands what matters to clients, and that's what they talk about. The fact that the most important work involves laying the foundation is not something a contractor bothers a client with.

For a long time, accounting could be the goal, the desired end result. The government demands accurate tax returns and records, and business owners and stakeholders need to understand the finances of their companies. Although that has remained unchanged, other things are changing dramatically. Thanks to technological developments, the financial foundation, maintaining financial records and filing returns, is done better, faster and at a lower cost than ever before. To top it off, less expertise is needed in that process. Most bookkeeping can be done by clients themselves, with no special accounting expertise required. It is almost as if the client lays the foundation of the house himself, and the contractor only steps in for the final touch.

What does it mean for you if accounting is not the goal, but the foundation? What does it mean for you if you cannot earn as much from "standard" work because clients use technology to lay a large part of the foundations themselves? You may conclude that you need a lot more clients to earn the same amount of money. That is a possibility. But I think there's another possibility. I think you can help your clients build their houses. I think you can help them make their businesses financially healthy and profitable.

If you are going to help your client build a healthy and profitable business, then you are no longer an accountant, but a profit advisor. You're not someone who just has to make sure that the legal and tax obligations are met as cheaply as possible, but someone who helps clients position their companies for success and profitability. This has several effects:

- You can use much more of your knowledge and skills, which should make your work more interesting.
- Your client seeks your advice in a broader area than just taxation and administration, which makes you more appreciated.
- Your client is willing to pay more for your services because you add more value.
- You need fewer clients to bring in the same (or even more) revenue, so you can pay more attention to your clients, add more value and be more appreciated.
- You are ahead of the crowd and stand out in the market. It is completely clear what you offer entrepreneurs and what value you add. You are less dependent on the standard accounting work, so you can secure your own future.

You may wonder: Does my client want a profit advisor? Can I fulfill that role? And how do I go about it? These are legitimate questions. You will find the answers to all these questions in this book.

1.2 Do entrepreneurs want a profit advisor?

Do clients want a profit advisor? In order to answer this question, I first zoom in on what clients don't want, and then bridge the gap to exploring what they do want.

In 2010, I gave my first workshop on finance for solopreneurs entitled "Financially conscious entrepreneurship." More than 200 entrepreneurs met at a national network meeting to attend workshops and meet new people. I was one of five speakers, so I expected about forty participants. I had prepared a good keynote, which would serve to raise entrepreneurs' financial awareness in an hour-and-a-half. I wanted to teach them the language of finance, because I know that it can help them find more success in their businesses. To my astonishment, of the 200 attendees, only five entrepreneurs were interested in finance. The others opted for more "flashy" topics, such as SEO, pitching and content marketing – topics that helped generate more clients and more sales. Revenue was their real interest.

I learned a very important lesson: entrepreneurs are not interested in finance. They think and say things like: "Numbers are boring, difficult and you can't do anything with them. Bookkeeping is a necessary evil. Accountants speak a language I don't understand. Bookkeeping knowledge doesn't help me; being able to read the annual accounts doesn't make me more money." Entrepreneurs don't think accounting is sexy. They don't connect it to their bottom line.

For years I kept responding to those "myths" with rational arguments. I explained to entrepreneurs that finance does matter to them. I argued that I could teach everyone to read annual accounts. I convinced them of the opposite: that understanding your numbers is essential to running a successful business. And that financial insight does help you earn more money, because it helps you make the right choices. It turns out, I was right on all those points. But being right is irrelevant. As long as I didn't really understand what entrepreneurs thought and what their perceptions of their problems were, we weren't speaking the same language. Until I learned to put myself in my clients' position, to really learn what mattered most to them, I didn't have a shot at convincing them that hiring me was a powerful choice for their businesses.

So, let's consider what the entrepreneur actually says:

1. Numbers are boring and difficult.

Many entrepreneurs have a deep dislike of finances. They don't really understand the stuff and certainly don't feel excited about it. I regularly meet entrepreneurs who say they clam up as soon as financial matters are discussed. The logical consequence is that they use their bookkeeper or accountant as an alibi. The entrepreneur "hires" an accountant and thus absolves himself of taking financial responsibility. And when we, the financial experts, explain that business owners need to understand their finances, they push back harder. "If I just do what I am good at, the money will come in naturally," and "everyone has his expertise" are frequently heard reactions. Really listening to the entrepreneur, though, does work. Acknowledging clients' fear of figures is a start. "I understand you," I often say. "Finance is a complicated matter. The tax system is downright complex. And we, financial experts, don't make things any easier with our technical jargon either." That recognition helps. Entrepreneurs feel like they've been heard, and that often creates room for a discussion about a difficult subject. If entrepreneurs feel understood, they dare to admit that they lie awake at night worrying about numbers. They worry about paying bills and taxes. Bookkeeping gives them headaches, because they're many months behind. Only after their real concerns and problems are acknowledged are clients ready and able to hear that I can help them build a financially healthy and profitable business.

2. I do not understand my accountant.

As an accountant, you are an expert in your specific field: finance. And because you are an expert, the language of accounting is second nature to you. Accruals, deferred income, journal entries, debits and current assets: these terms are your native tongue, but for the average entrepreneur, these words are as incomprehensible as Martian.

Finance is the universal language of business. With rare exceptions, your clients don't speak or understand that language. For them, a balance sheet and profit and loss account are what the book Programming in C++ is for a non-programmer: a lot of numbers without any coherence.

I regularly speak to accountants who believe that their clients do actually understand the language of finance. Their clients are intelligent and have revenues in the hundreds of thousands, or even millions of dollars annually. These misguided accountants fervently believe these entrepreneurs could never have come so far without financial knowledge. Based on my years of experience, I dare to say that these accountants are in for a rude awakening. If they take the time to really learn how much (or little) their clients know about finance, they're likely to be shocked. Make sure you and your clients speak the same language.

3. I don't see how financial insight helps make more money.

Average entrepreneurs – the ones who don't speak the language of finance – have no idea how much valuable information is contained in their companies' numbers and that these numbers contain the only truth about their businesses. Knowing and understanding the truth gives your clients the tools to earn more money, sleep better and work fewer hours.

When you limit yourself to reporting on the past, the entrepreneur almost has a point.

Almost, because I do know that information about the past contains a lot of relevant and valuable insights for the future. But I agree with many entrepreneurs that the past is not as interesting as the present or the future. Entrepreneurship is about innovation, about leading the market, about responding directly to what is important and what is happening. In order to make yourself relevant to your client, you must translate your expertise in terms of the future health and prosperity of your client's business.

Annual accounts from one-and-a-half years ago fall into the category of "prehistoric information." An entrepreneur really can't do anything with that, and it's a waste of time and money to study it.

But even if you're a modern accountant who works in the cloud and ensures that clients always have access to real-time information, those clients still don't know what to do with this information. Most entrepreneurs do keep an eye on their revenue and pay some attention to their margin, especially in the trade or retail sector. But that's about it. You see everything your clients are missing. You see that entrepreneurs lose a lot of money because of poor credit management, or that costs are too high for their revenue level, and those costs continue to rise. You have the information and knowledge to help your clients earn more and sleep better. You know what can save your clients from bankruptcy. By understanding your clients' needs and helping them to understand how your skills as a profit advisor can save their businesses, you're taking the first steps toward profitability... for both you and your clients.

Conclusion: entrepreneurs do not want to learn the language of finance.

At that first keynote, I learned that average entrepreneurs don't want to learn everything about the financial foundation of their companies. They do feel the pain of being financially illiterate, but they're in denial and unable to take action. They don't see the benefit of learning the language of finance. Financial literacy is too much work for too little gain, at least in most business owners' minds. And that poorly attended keynote marked the moment that I realized I needed to start working on creating awareness. I thought that by making finance fun, practical and accessible, I could bridge that gap. And I partly succeeded. In the years that followed, I supported thousands of entrepreneurs in building their financially healthy businesses. I did that by breaking down finances to the very basics, by speaking in simple, concrete terms and by giving examples about their businesses instead of explaining boring, abstract theory. And that worked... to a certain extent.

It still took many years before I could really meet the needs of the entrepreneur, before I fully realized that accounting is genuinely a foundation, an element that's vital, but that no one wants to talk about in detail. I realized entrepreneurs need other tools to become successful.

Do entrepreneurs want a profit advisor?

Now back to my question: Do entrepreneurs want a profit advisor? The answer to that question is a resounding "Yes!" When I started to listen to entrepreneurs and heard what their real problems and challenges were, I discovered that they did have financial issues. And these issues weren't theoretical. They were very practical. They didn't want to know how to read annual accounts; they just wanted to know what prices to charge for their products and how to make more profit. They didn't want to learn how the tax system works; they just didn't want to lie awake at night worrying about how much they owed in taxes. They didn't want to draw up a cash flow statement, but they did want to manage their cash.

Should you stop doing your clients' bookkeeping and tax returns? Absolutely not, but you need to recognize that's just the foundation. The books need to be in order and cost as little time, money and effort as possible. The time, money and energy freed up can be devoted to the entrepreneur's real goal: to make a profit, be successful, happy, and make the world a better place.

1.3 Innovations in accounting

Financial specialists have historically had plenty of well-paid work as a result of laws and regulations. Worldwide there are millions of companies whose accounting and annual accounts must comply with legal standards and regulations. Tax authorities impose requirements on accounting and reporting, as do Chambers of Commerce and other governmental agencies. GAAP and IFRS impose hundreds, if not thousands of standards and regulations on us to ensure that our figures are timely, reliable and comparable.

These requirements automatically created a lot of work for financial specialists, but the industry changes and moves fast. Important developments include cloud accounting, mobile accounting, linked bank accounts, scanning and recognition software, robotic accounting, self-learning software, Artificial Intelligence, UBL, XML, XBRL, PSD$_2$, SBR, RCSFI, and Blockchain. These and other accounting innovations reduce manual accounting work, help provide near real-time information and improve coordination between entrepreneurs and their accountant or bookkeeper. Whether we like it or not, technology has an impact on your firm.

Below is a brief explanation of several important technological developments.

SaaS/Cloud

Thanks to SaaS (*Software as a Service*), you no longer need to purchase an accounting application. Entrepreneurs and accounting firms only pay for the use of the online software in the cloud. The software provider takes care of timely updates and regular backups. Both entrepreneurs and their financial advisors have access to the accounts, which allows optimal coordination and weekly or even daily updates.

Mobile accounting

Online accounting programs are often supported by an app. Entrepreneurs can use this app to scan receipts, so they are directly added to the bookkeeping system. The app often also contains a convenient dashboard, which allows entrepreneurs to glance at their mobile phones to see how their business is doing. These features require that accounts are updated on a daily or weekly basis.

Linked bank accounts

Often accounting software is automatically linked to the company's bank account. As a result, all bank transactions from the previous day are recorded in the accounts every morning. These do not then need to be imported or entered manually. There are even real-time links with some banks.

Scan and recognition functions

Accounting software with a scan and recognition function uses OCR (*Optical Character Recognition*). The software "reads" the invoice and makes its own entry proposal based on it.

Robotic accounting

Robotic accounting means that the computer takes over tasks from people. For example, accounting software often automatically processes bank statements. Thanks to developments in robotic accounting, we can expect that accounting will increasingly be taken over by computers.

Self-learning software

Modern accounting software "learns" to make the right entries itself. When a transaction (bank entry or invoice) has been processed before, the software automatically proposes a journal entry.

E-invoicing

Electronic invoicing (e-invoicing) is faster, cheaper, easier and more accurate. Many international small businesses are taking advantage of e-invoicing through platforms such as Quickbooks Online. An e-invoice is a digital (XML) file with a fixed structure.

UBL

UBL, *Universal Business Language*, is a standard electronic language that can be used in financial documents. An XML file is created with a document, in which all information about that document is stored. The XML file has a universal format, meaning that it can be "read" by any program that uses UBL. UBL is, for example, used when sending a sales invoice. If the receiving party also uses UBL, the invoice can be processed fully automatically.

SBR

SBR, *Standard Business Reporting*, is the Dutch national standard for the digital exchange of all business reports. Australia and New Zealand have worked in accordance with the SBR method for many years and a growing number of countries are interested in the Dutch SBR approach. With SBR, the data in the financial administration is recorded once in a standard manner. With one push of a button, reports are prepared and sent digitally to various parties. Parties (including governments) need to spend less effort to prepare and supply various mandatory reports.[1]

RCSFI

RCSFI stands for *Reference Classification System of Financial Information*. RCSFI establishes a link between the client's chart of accounts and Standard Business Reporting. By linking the own classification to the standard classification system, data can be retrieved and reported easily and more quickly according to the standard classification.[2]

XML audit files

An XML audit file (XML stands for *eXtensible Markup Language*) is an open standard for storing and/or exchanging data from administrative systems, such as accounting and payroll software. With the help of an audit file, data can be exported from one package and imported into another package.

PSD2

PSD2 (*Payment Service Directive*) and its predecessor PSD aim to create a uniform payment market within the European Union. This should make cross-border payments as easy, efficient and secure as domestic payments. Thanks to PSD2, banks can share account information with third parties in real time, depending, of course, on your authorization and permission. With PSD2 you can also perform a balance check before cashing an invoice.

Blockchain

Blockchain was developed in 2009 as the system on which Bitcoin runs. But there is so much more you can do with blockchain than just trade in cryptocurrency. Blockchain technology is all about recording transactions in a digital ledger. This means that not only do the transferring parties (two companies, authorities, consumers, etc.) register a transaction, but that the transaction is also recorded in a distributed network.

A lot of information is kept in databases, for example, identity data or medical records. We know how much money each person owns, because the banks keep all financial transactions in a database or general ledger. The big disadvantage of our current databases is that they run centrally. Someone, an agency or government, is responsible for it and we must trust that the owner of the database handles our data properly and securely. With blockchain, this dependence on an authority or government is not there. Blockchain is about a shared digital truth and about trust. Information becomes tamper-proof and, in principle, invulnerable.

1.4 The significance of these developments for the profession

The above developments are neither complete nor static. There will be many more developments in the coming months and years, and we will see several important implications for bookkeepers and accountants. What is likely to happen as a result of these developments?

Lower prices

One important consequence of these innovations is that prices for accounting services are dropping. As work becomes automated, prices are reduced. We see these lower prices already, and they are certain to spread. Accounting firms that do not keep up with automation will become too expensive, and clients will switch to competitors who ask less for the same result.

Higher demands

Clients quickly get used to the new reality. It won't be long before they expect accounts to be updated immediately, all the time. As accounting becomes more automated, clients will expect more services for their money.

The client does the bookkeeping himself

Another implication of automation is that the clients believe they can handle their books themselves. Historically, entrepreneurs who wanted to do their own bookkeeping had to learn two things: double-entry bookkeeping and working with bookkeeping software developed for accountants. These were not impossible challenges, but still the vast majority of entrepreneurs did not want to take up those challenges.

Accounting software for solopreneurs and SMEs are now widely available. These packages claim that you can do the books without knowing the trade of bookkeeping.

QuickBooks Online, FreshBooks, Xero, Zoho Books, and Wave Financial are just some examples. This software answers the two challenges I mentioned above: entrepreneurs don't have to learn double-entry bookkeeping and the software is intuitive, so entrepreneurs can start immediately without training. Entrepreneurs have seized this opportunity en masse.

So why would entrepreneurs suddenly want to do their own accounting? That is a legitimate question. The accounting software for solopreneurs and SMEs is a response to a common complaint from entrepreneurs that accounting costs too much time, money and energy. With an entrepreneur-friendly online system, they can easily create invoices, which are then processed straight away. Business owners can easily store purchase invoices and can quickly send reminders. The real motivation is not to outsource bookkeeping, but to make bookkeeping less of a hassle. If a solution allows entrepreneurs to do everything without having to know anything about bookkeeping, then the choice is easy. They do it themselves. The accountant may keep an eye on things behind the scenes and prepare the end-of-year returns, but business owners certainly don't want to pay too much for that service. After all, they're doing most of the work themselves.

And that is where the big challenge for today's bookkeeper arises. The client chooses his own package, makes sure that 90% of the transactions are processed and asks you to do the end-of-year work for a pittance. How does an accountant earn a living under these new circumstances?

Action step

Consider the following questions: "To what extent do I make use of modern technologies?" and "In which areas do I already fulfill the role of profit advisor for my client, and in which areas am I still lacking?"

The aim of this first chapter was to give you an overview of the developments in the field and your role in them. In Chapter 2, we will make the transition to your mission and vision and how they form the foundation of your future.

---

1. Source: https://www.sbr-nl.nl/sbr-international
2. For more information: https://www.referentiegrootboekschema.nl/english

2 YOUR MISSION AND VISION

* * *

People don't buy what you do. They buy why you do it –
Simon Sinek

* * *

Before my appointment with Peter's accountant, Greg, I took a look at his firm's website. I read sentences like:

"Dedicated, reliable and committed Experts.
One stop solution for all your bookkeeping needs.
You manage your business, we take care of the books."

Just empty words – you could read the same words on the website of any other firm. Those words told me nothing about who Greg was and what he had to offer Peter or his other clients.

I hoped that Greg's business was doing so well that it was not necessary to use his website to spread his message. But given Peter's stories, I feared that Greg himself did not know exactly what his vision was and why he was doing what he was doing.

* * *

The financial world is changing. Your profession is changing. The meaning of this new reality is different for everyone, but in the end everyone will have to move forward. To know what your new reality looks like, you must have clarity about where you are now, what drives you and where you want to go. Without that vision you will get lost in an ocean of possibilities. You will aimlessly make choices, look at competitors, randomly add or remove products and, by doing so, you will confuse your clients.

2.1 Where are you now?

Most accountants will recognize themselves in one of the descriptions below.

1. *We are in the middle of a transformation.*

Many accountants are in the process of transforming into the accounting firm of the future. Working online is the standard. All manual work is replaced by digital accounting.

The owners of these firms face two major basic challenges:

– *The client doesn't want to change.* Some clients are happy with how things are. They collect their receipts and hand them in. But is this model sustainable? In the end, it costs you too much time and money to keep working this way. You will need to seduce the client into joining you in your new way of working.

– *How should we earn our money now?* Another problem is that automation makes it more difficult to make good money with compliancy work, with bookkeeping basics. Smart accountants realize they need to start selling more advisory services, but there needs to be a demand. Chapters 3 through 7 will demonstrate that the demand has existed for a long time. You will learn how to identify this client's need and how to link it to your business model.

2. *We are not there yet*

There are also accountants who haven't yet caught up with technology. Maybe you are actually quite satisfied with how things are going now, and you don't believe things will change so fast. It is possible that this book will open your eyes. It may inspire you to think about your role. How could a different way of working contribute to your vision of the accounting profession? How could another role help you achieve your personal and business goals? And how could you serve your clients even better?

Take a moment to ask yourself where you stand today.

2.2 What drives you?

Whatever your situation, your new role brings challenges. To solve these challenges, you must reflect on your mission and vision. If you know where you stand, you can think about what your company of the future looks like.

There are at least two essential questions every entrepreneur should be able to answer:

1. Why do I do what I do?

2. Where am I going?

The answer to the first question is probably close to your mission statement. It is your why, your company's raison d'être. It gives meaning to what you do. The answer to question two tells you about your vision. It's about what you, from your Why, want to achieve in the long term.

Chances are you already asked yourself these questions when you started your business. Most entrepreneurs, in addition to the desire to have more freedom or earn more money, have a higher goal in mind with their business; there is something important you want to achieve. That may not have been possible in your job and that's why you decided to create it yourself.

Your mission and vision together form your drive. This drive is incredibly important. Your drive helps you through times of adversity – because there is a higher goal. Your drive also helps you determine your direction; it is your spot on the horizon, that point you keep your eye on to ensure you're going the right way. Thanks to your drive you and your team know what to do and it motivates everyone to achieve results. Your drive is also one of the most important foundations of your marketing message and sales pitch. People buy from people. Without your drive, your vision and your mission, you are just another company, just another cog in a machine.

Based on your mission and vision, you formulate your objectives and create your strategy. This is the long-term answer to the question of how to achieve these objectives. Your strategy will then guide your plan for this year, this quarter, this week and this moment. Objectives, strategies and plans are discussed in Chapter 11.

2.3 Mission: The Why of your company

Your company's raison d'etre is about what's essential to you, what you believe in and why you do what you do. Your mission often originates in your past and indicates that what you do has a meaning that goes beyond accounting. Simon Sinek explains this powerfully using The Golden Circle (see Figure 1) in his book and TedTalk, *Start with Why*.

According to Sinek, accountants prioritize what they do and that is what comes first in their various communications: conversations, websites, brochures. They explain, "I am an accountant and I make sure that the accounts are reconciled and that the tax returns are filed on time." The how is generally also given enough attention. It's about how financial specialists provide services and how they distinguish themselves from others: "We work fully online, so the client always has access to the numbers." Or, "We take care of the finances, so that the entrepreneur can focus on his core business." The accountant's why is barely mentioned, and that's a shame because your Why creates an impact. Your Why touches people's hearts. Your Why inspires and creates a connection. Your Why builds Know, Like and Trust (your client will like you, trust you and wants to do business with you). Your Why is the core of everything you do and the energy that fires you up.

So, Sinek advises, "Turn it around and start with your Why!" A message could then sound, for example, as follows: "I believe that everyone is responsible for creating their own success. A company is a great vehicle to make your dreams come true and achieve your goals. This requires a financially healthy and profitable business (Why). I make finances fun, practical and accessible, so that every entrepreneur can build a financially healthy and profitable business (How). I provide training, give keynotes and I write books (What)."

Your Why is already there. You don't have to create it; you just have to find it. The best way to find your Why is by asking a series of questions.

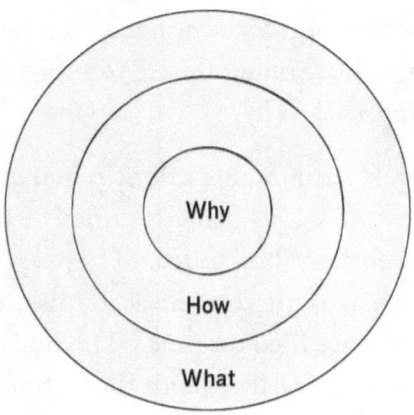

Figure 1: *The Golden Circle*

1. Why do you do what you do?
2. Why is ... important? (Fill in your answer to question 1 in the gap.)
3. Why is ... important? (Fill in your answer to question 2 in the gap.)
4. Why is ... important? (Fill in your answer to question 3 in the gap.)
5. Why is ... important? (Fill in your answer to question 4 in the gap.)

Sometimes it is necessary to ask this question[1] four or five times, sometimes even up to seven times. It can help to alternate the question "Why is ... important" with the questions "How does ... benefit you?" or "What does ... mean to you?" These slightly different questions can give you new insights. Take your time answering these questions and know that the answer is already there. You won't have to invent or create anything.

You can ask these questions yourself or ask someone else to help you. In any case, take the time and space to do this important work. Turn off your phone and email for a few hours or go for a walk in the woods.

The advantage of asking a third party to help you is that the other person can write down your answers for you and ask you the question just a little differently (see the example sentences above), which may make it easier for you to retrieve your Why. However, it is important to do this with someone who will refrain from doing anything other than asking questions. This exercise is counterproductive when a person helps with giving the answers or reformulates or interprets your answers for you.

Communicating about your Why

Having a clear mission is fantastic. You experience your Why in everything you do and if you don't, it is often a signal that you are not doing the right things. Although knowing your why is an important goal in itself, it is not enough. Communicating your why to your team, your client and other stakeholders is at least as important. Your mission may have a prominent place on your website and in your company brochure, but also in job advertisements and on social media. And if you're talking to potential clients at a networking meeting or a birthday, experiment with Simon Sinek's advice: "Start with Why." When someone asks: "What do you do?" don't tell them straightaway that you are an accountant (because honestly, many entrepreneurs will quickly run away), but start with your Why. Chances are, after hearing your why, the person you are talking will be excited to hear what you do!

2.4 Vision: Where are you going?

Your vision is about what you, based on your Why, want to achieve with your company in the long term. It is a dream of the future, an ambitious goal, aimed at making big changes that matter to you. A vision can be grand, impressive and even a little unattainable or vague. A vision does not need to be fixed but may develop over the years.

The non-profit organization, War Child's vision: "A world in which no child's life is torn apart by war," speaks for itself. And although it is, unfortunately, not achievable at the moment, it clearly indicates where War Child wants to go and what principles drive War Child.

About 40 years ago, Bill Gates' vision was: "A computer on every desk and in every home." This seemed impossible at the time, but it eventually made Microsoft a multinational corporation.

My vision is for all entrepreneurs in the Netherlands and Belgium to have a financially healthy and profitable company. For now, this vision gives me plenty of room to run multiple companies and do great things. Who knows, someday I might replace the Netherlands and Belgium with Europe.

A clear vision offers you the tools to make choices and steer your company in the right direction at any moment. A vision is inspiring. You know what you are doing it for, and that motivates you and your team and gives you the energy to work toward the same goal. Without a vision you're rudderless; you will float and meander from left to right. Your team members will lose motivation and start underperforming. Your potential client will be confused about where exactly you are going and will quit.

Some entrepreneurs are crystal clear about their vision and feature that vision prominently in all their branding and messaging. Other entrepreneurs once had a vision but have lost track of it over the years. And still others have never really thought much about it.

If you don't have a clear vision, and you feel that it is necessary to take the next step toward more profit, better clients and more free time, then go through the steps below, by yourself or with your team:

- *Start from your mission*

Remember your Why. Look at the world and your immediate surroundings with your mission in mind. What will the world look like in ten or twenty years? What does the world look like when you fulfill your mission? What do you want to have achieved by that time?

- *Explore industry developments*

Look at the developments in your industry. What trends do you see? Do these trends impact your vision? What opportunities do you see and how do you want to respond to them? What threats do you perceive and how do you deal with them? What changes do you notice in the needs of clients? By exploring the developments, you will get a better insight into where you want to go.

- *Make choices*

When thinking about your vision, you need to make tough choices. You can only sail in one direction, so when you choose your spot on the horizon you are necessarily excluding other possibilities.

- *Make your vision short, powerful and attractive*

When formulating your vision, you must make sure it is short and powerful, and that it makes you hungry. Hearing or reading your vision should give you, your team and other shareholders a "YES feeling." Take note of these five conditions when formulating your vision:

1. Positive – Avoid words like "not" and "none," but express what you do want: "We make use of the latest technologies," instead of "We are not a receipt-processing factory."

2. As if now – Avoid words like "want", "maybe" and "possible." Make it seem as if it has already happened: "We are an organization that..." instead of "We want to be an organization that..."

3. Ambitious – Your vision may be grand and ambitious. A vision that lacks ambition is boring. People shrug their shoulders and move on to business as usual. As soon as ambition is expressed in a vision, it inspires. People stop what they are doing and think about what it means to them. An ambitious vision leads to results. "All entrepreneurs in the Netherlands" is more exciting than "entrepreneurs".

4. Specific to your company – Although your vision may be a bit vague and seem unattainable, it's important that it is about your company, and not about any other firm in the city. Only when your vision is clearly about your company will your team members remember and learn your vision and inspire potential clients with it. "We help entrepreneurs with their finances" is too general. "We make finance fun, practical and accessible, so that our clients can build a financially healthy business," is much more personal.

5. Future-oriented – It is obvious that a vision is about something that has yet to happen, that it articulates goals yet to be attained. This can be expressed by linking a year (2040) or a time period (in twenty years) to your vision, but even without mentioning a year, it can be clear from the formulation that it is about a vision for the future. When I say: "All entrepreneurs in the Netherlands and Belgium have a financially healthy and profitable company," it is clear to everyone that what I picture isn't the current situation, but a desired future.

Communicating your vision

Just like your mission, your vision deserves a prominent place in your communications. Don't hesitate to share your vision in conversations, at network meetings, on your website, in your company brochure, during job interviews and in team meetings. I'm surprised at how often we forget the latter.

We believe our teams already know our vision, so we neglect to reinforce it. But if your team members aren't regularly reminded of the company vision, it will eventually disappear from their thoughts, and they will have no drive to achieve exactly what you want them to achieve. They will be missing your spot on the horizon, and they may steer toward some other goal. They may lack a level of ambition that could give them that extra push. You should communicate your vision so often that it becomes part of your company's DNA, ensuring that every action is always driven by the same guiding force.

Action step

Formulate your mission and vision. Are your mission and vision entirely clear to you? Look at how you communicate your mission and vision. Can you do better? If you are not entirely clear on your mission and vision, set aside half a day to reflect. Open your planner right now. If you don't schedule this, it won't happen.

In this chapter I presented you with tools to formulate your mission and vision. Your vision and mission form the foundation of your work. You can't build a great future on a weak foundation.

Chapter 3 is about a fundamental question: What is your client's real problem and what solution do you offer?

---

1. This method is known as the "five times why"-method and is developed by Sakichi Toyoda, the founder of Toyota Industries. Toyoda used this method to get to the cause of a problem as well as its solution.

3 DELIVER RESULTS, NOT ACTIONS

* * *

Sell the problem you solve, not the product – Source unknown

* * *

On a drizzly Tuesday morning I drove into a shopping center somewhere in the east of the country. Finally. It had not been easy to make an appointment with Greg. Several times I was told: "Something has come up." There had been no response to my request to send some reports in advance. I wasn't very happy, because we still didn't have any insight into the financial situation of Peter's company.

The accountant's office was located above a clothing store. Peter and I were slightly early. Before we rang the bell, I stopped Peter and asked him: "What do you see as the most important issue?"

Peter looked surprised. "Well, just that," he said, "the figures must be in order."

"And then?" I asked. "Is that enough?"

Peter thought long and hard. And when he started talking, I heard a tremble in his voice. "What I really want," he began, "is to make enough money with my business. So that I don't have discussions with my wife about money on Friday evening at ten o'clock. So, I don't stare at the ceiling when everyone else in the country is already asleep. I want there to be enough money to do grocery shopping, pay for my staff, make the right investments and occasionally have something left over for a holiday or eating out. And there's something else," he added. "I do not want to have any more stress about the accounts and taxes. It would be nice if those things just worked, without causing any stress." He was silent for a while, and then said, "But I can't put all that on Greg's plate, can I? Surely that is far too much for an accountant?"

"Well, perhaps for a traditional accountant," I replied. "But for a profit advisor, your challenge is child's play."

* * *

The first chapter contained four messages:

1. Accounting is the foundation, not the goal. Books need to be in order, but that should take as little time, money and energy as possible.

2. Because of automation you will earn less and less with basic accounting work. Increasingly these tasks will be done by the computer or by clients themselves.

3. If you, as an accountant, want to continue to earn money, you

will have to add value that goes beyond the standard work. You will have to become a profit advisor.

4. As a profit advisor, you go deeper. You add more value, and you can ask higher prices and earn more with less effort.

The first step toward becoming a profit advisor is to take a new look at what your client needs and what you offer him. Traditionally accountants, like lawyers, work reactively and invoice the hours worked. If clients ask a question, they get an answer. If they remain quiet and don't submit any receipts, the books will not be updated. If the clients are really inefficient and fail to submit half of the receipts, reply only to some emails or reply too late, ask the same question several times (even if they are already answered), then the average accountant has no real problem with that. It may be annoying, but, after all, the client is paying for the inefficiency.

Here lies both your opportunity and your challenge. This traditional, reactive way of working was fine when accounting was still the goal. But now that accounting is the foundation and having a successful and profitable business is the goal, you need new strategies. You are no longer asked to deliver tasks (processing information after it has been supplied), but to deliver results (such as real-time insight into figures, peace of mind concerning the taxes to be paid, more profit). It is expected that you commit yourself to your client's results and that you take a proactive role in delivering those results.

In order to deliver results, you need to know who your clients are, what they want, what problems you are solving for them and how you plan to solve those problems. This chapter helps you get to those answers. In the following chapters, I will zoom in on the profitable services you can offer, along with sales strategies for your valuable new services.

3.1 What is your client's real problem?

Since we agree that "doing the books" is not so much the ultimate goal of your collaboration, but rather a component that should take minimal time, energy and money, a logical question arises: What actually is your goal?

To be able to answer that question, you first must figure out which problems you want to solve. My working definition of an enterprise is: *"a driven, profitable organization which sells a solution to solve the client's problem and delivers this solution as efficiently as possible."*

In Chapter 11, I will discuss this definition in more detail, but for now it is important to understand that as a financial specialist you can only run a successful, profitable company if you know what the client's problem is, so that you can solve it in an efficient way.

Some problems are obvious. Your client cannot do accounting and has no knowledge of tax matters. Problem identified. But there is so much more... How often do you look at a client's figures with amazement and think, "How on earth is it possible that ...?" That happens when you've identified a problem. Maybe your client clearly never thought about the cost price of his goods and has margins that are unsustainably low. Or perhaps the one service that used to generate the most revenue is no longer popular. Or the outstanding receivables keep on increasing. Or no pension is built up. Or the tax liability is increasing. Or there is still no room to pay out a salary. Or personal expenses keep coming out of business accounts. Or...

These are problems you have identified before, probably even mentioned a few times, but since your client hasn't taken any action, in the end you just stop mentioning them. It has become the status quo.

And then there are the underlying problems, which are the real cause of the misery. One client is afraid of numbers. Another doesn't know where to start. Others think they're bad at numbers and bury their heads in the sand. We are talking about finance, about money: a subject that every entrepreneur, every human being, must deal with on a daily basis. Finance evokes fear and emotion. Everyone needs money, yet a large proportion of people claim that money doesn't make them happy. A company that doesn't make a profit cannot survive, yet many entrepreneurs claim that they don't have to make a profit. Because of all these emotions and beliefs, entrepreneurs earn significantly less and lose far more sleep than they should. And you don't have to be a psychologist to help them with this.

This book offers you practical tools to help your client on these deeper levels. First, it is important to get as clear a picture as possible of your clients' real problems.

How do you identify your clients' problems?

An obvious way is to ask. But as soon as you start asking how you can help your clients even better and which problems still need to be solved, there is a good chance that the answers are either not entirely honest or incomplete. Maybe your clients don't understand what you really want, or they don't want to criticize your services. Simply asking surface questions is unlikely to yield the answers you really need.

Ask entrepreneurs outside of your own circle of clients.

Instead of asking your own clients, it is probably better – especially if you are still in the inventory phase – to start with entrepreneurs who are not your client and not likely ever to become one. You can ask them what you want without any risk or emotions! Go to a network meeting or use the opportunity when you meet an entrepreneur at a birthday party or in the schoolyard. You will notice that entrepreneurs always like to answer questions about doing business, and these conversations often lead to insights for both you and the business owner!

If you want to discover what entrepreneurs' real problems and challenges are, you can ask them the following questions:

- What frustrates you about the accounting industry?
- What would you like accountants to do differently?
- What should change so that bookkeeping will take you less energy?
- What confuses you the most in the accounting profession?
- What services or products would you like to buy from accountants that you can't buy now?
- What is your biggest financial challenge?

Join forums or Facebook groups

You can also get a lot of information by listening carefully to questions entrepreneurs ask in public. On LinkedIn as well as on Facebook and other forums, there are countless business groups where entrepreneurs ask for help with all facets of entrepreneurship. Financial questions are also frequently asked. Search for groups that contain your ideal client and read along! You can, of course, also answer questions there, which will bring you to the attention of your target group. But since at this stage you mainly want to discover what frustrates and worries entrepreneurs, you can also limit yourself to reading along.

Put yourself in your clients' position

In the end, you don't want to know every entrepreneur's problems; you want to know your client's problems. Of course, you don't constantly question whether you're meeting every possible client need. Some days, you just do their accounting. But if, on the other hand, you never think about what the client really needs, you will not develop, refine and improve your services and products. Without a desire to improve and better meet client needs, you risk losing both existing and potential clients.

It is important to regularly look past your current services and put yourself in the clients' shoes. Find out what their worries and challenges are. What keeps them awake at night? What do they worry about? What do they yearn for? What do they dream of? Ask them questions when you are meeting them.

Make it a habit to have an annual meeting. This doesn't have to take place in December, the month in which the end-of-year meetings traditionally take place, but it can also take place in the summer, when there's a good chance both you and your client will have more time for it!

For example, ask your client the following questions:

- Where do you want to be in five or ten years?
- Where do you want to be one year from now?
- What is the biggest obstacle to getting there?
- How does your bookkeeping help or hinder you in this?
- How do you think I could help you achieve your goals?
- What is your biggest concern when it comes to your finances?
- Suppose I gave you a magic wand and with just one flick you were able to organize your bookkeeping any way you want. What would your bookkeeping look like then? This seems like a dangerous question, because your client may wish for the impossible. But the effect of this question is that it will make your client think

beyond self-defined frameworks and boundaries and provide you with useful information.
- What do you dream of? If anything were possible, what would you do? This question seems rather cheeky, because what does this have to do with your role? However, this question will help connect your client to his bigger dreams and deeper desires and getting those dreams out in the open can produce major effects. I remember asking a client this question, and after a short silence she said: "I want to buy a castle in France. I want my husband to cook there while I organize retreats." We always returned to this dream in our daily actions. We opened a separate bank account, so that she could structurally set aside money for this purpose. But we also looked at how she could already make it happen. Thanks to our efforts, she managed to organize, for the first time, a retreat in a castle in France the following summer. It's not yet her castle, but by structurally setting aside money for her dream every month and by organizing a retreat now, she's making sure that her dream isn't farfetched, but is a very real spot on the horizon, a horizon she's actively working and saving for. Understanding a client's dreams helps you take action to make them very real.

You can't find out what your client's real problem is in ten minutes. It's also not something you'll just work with once and then never revisit. You should regularly return to this topic to keep improving your services. By looking for the real problems and dreams of your clients and the entrepreneurs you meet, you will get a clearer picture of the problems you enjoy solving and are good at solving. You will discover what your "ideal" problem is. You are going to develop a solution for it. In Chapter 7 you will also learn to conduct the sales conversation so your very first discussion with clients will get to the core of their problems, allowing you to offer the right solution for the right price.

3.2 What is the real solution?

Once you know your client's problem, you must start looking for the real solution. The major challenge is to describe the solution in terms of results and effects, rather than in terms of actions, activities or processes. Experts are accustomed to talking in terms of processes. We do the accounting in program X, Y or Z, we take care of the tax returns via our tax preparation software and we do the payroll administration via our payroll partner. That all sounds fine, but these are often not the solutions that the client is really looking for. Your client probably doesn't care how the payroll administration is done and is definitely not interested in which program or with which partner. Your client just wants his or her staff to receive the right amount of money on time every month.

At first sight it may sound like the same thing, but it's not. Because even if you or your payroll partner do payroll correctly and on time, it is still not a guarantee that the entrepreneur can pay the salaries on time. Certainly not if – and this seems like an annual surprise to some clients—vacation pay is due. "Hold on," I hear you think. "That's not my responsibility, is it?" Right now, I want to challenge you to think outside the box. Because these are exactly the solutions that entrepreneurs are looking for: They want to be able to pay themselves and their staff on time. They don't want to worry about finding money to pay taxes. They want fewer discussions with their partners about money. They don't' want to think about the process or the foundation. They want the results, and they need your expertise to achieve them.

If you succeed in identifying your client's real problem, you will notice that the solutions often lie outside the field of traditional accounting. But accounting is the entry you can use to help your clients see the effects they desire. If, instead of selling activities to your clients, you start selling results, they will be much more inclined to work with you. And they will also be willing to pay a premium.

Let's be honest. What would you prefer? Someone who files your tax return for you or someone who ensures that you never have to lie awake at night again because of the taxes you must pay? Would you prefer someone who takes care of your payroll, or someone who helps you ensure that your staff is always paid on time? Do you want someone who does accounting for you, or someone who helps you always make a profit?

This is not a cheap marketing trick. These are not empty words. The intention is that you help your client to achieve these results. Then you are a profit advisor and you will be paid as a profit advisor.

To describe the results that the clients will achieve with your help, it is useful to look at important areas of their lives.

What results does your client achieve in cooperation with you in the following areas of life?

Security/safety

Every human being needs security and safety, an area where finance plays an important role. Financial concerns can create a lot of uncertainty and insecurity. Think of a client who hasn't set aside money for taxes, a client who has barely built up a pension or one who receives such a meager salary from his company that he cannot pay for rent or groceries. But also think of entrepreneurs who don't understand their figures or are months behind with the accounting. They, too, feel insecure about finances.

These are not unique examples. We all have stories of clients with problems like these, which isn't surprising. Unfortunately, hidden poverty is all too common among entrepreneurs. In fact, we see more than five times as much poverty among self-employed people as among traditional employees. Almost 10% of the self-employed live below the poverty line, while this is 1.7% for the employed. Entrepreneurs with staff are three times more likely to live in poverty as employees.[1] These facts must not be ignored. Are you responsible for solving this problem? No, I don't think so. But can you make a positive contribution? I'm sure you can.

How do you market the results clients can obtain while working with you on the area of financial safety and security? You can help them:

- Always put aside enough money to pay taxes.
- Secure their salary.
- Always pay their staff's salary on time.
- Have enough money for later.
- Use insight into figures to actively steer toward profit.

Health

A second important area of life where money plays a role is health – especially in causing or preventing stress. Money is an important stress factor, and research (including by researchers at Harvard and Princeton) has shown that people's thinking is impaired by financial worries. This also means that financial concerns can have a negative effect on entrepreneurs' ability to innovate and keep their business running.

You can help improve your clients' health by:

- Preventing worry and sleep loss over their ability to pay taxes.
- Encouraging them to dedicate one minute a day to their bookkeeping, plus an extra 30 minutes a week.
- Preparing them to file their tax return in one minute.
- Creating stress-free accounting.

Relationships

Many marital disputes are about money. And if one of the partners is an entrepreneur, money is undoubtedly a regular topic of conversation. Every time the entrepreneur fails to make a sufficient contribution to the family housekeeping budget, this causes unrest in the relationship. The partner will then often ask questions about the revenue, the operating costs or the budget. Entrepreneurs who lack insight into these figures – because they ignore them, because their accounts have not been updated, because they don't understand financial statements, you name it – will not have answers to these questions. The lack of information doesn't help. As soon as entrepreneurs understand their figures, they can give their partners clarity, which alleviates tension.

Help clients reduce relationship friction by:

- Encouraging daily account updates so they always have real-time insight into their numbers.

Identity/status

Having a profitable company often conveys a higher status, creating a feeling of pride. I know that from my own experience. I think making a profit is the best, because for me that is proof of a successful company. I am able to create something out of nothing. How cool is that? The fact that I (together with my husband) take care of the family income makes me proud too.

Results that you can market are, for example:

- Always making a profit.
- Making 10% more profit.
- Making a profitable plan and achieving goals.

Spirituality/growth

Many entrepreneurs are serving a higher purpose with their business. They want to create something, improve the world and help people. Unfortunately, I hear too many business owners claim that their focus isn't on making money or making a profit because they have loftier goals. Those entrepreneurs are missing a huge opportunity, because it is precisely by earning more money that they can invest more, reach more people and contribute more. Money can be a wonderful lever to achieve their spiritual goals.

Client results in this area may be:

- Achieving goals through a profitable company.
- Improve the world through a profitable business.
- Consistently reserving a portion of profit to donate to charity.

3.3 Who is your ideal client?

You know what your clients' real problems are and what results they want to achieve in cooperation with you. In order to deliver the most value, with as little effort as possible, it is important that you know exactly who your ideal client is.

Financial experts are often not very picky. Apart from several substantive specializations (self-employed, SMEs, Inc., tax advice, and others), everyone is welcome. After all, accounting is accounting. And yet... if you think carefully about it, that probably isn't quite the case. How often does a client knock on your door looking for help with an issue that makes you think: "Oh ... I'll have to study that first!" Or a client works with software you have no experience with? If you accept all the work that comes your way without asking yourself what you prefer to do and for whom, you create a lot of – mostly unpaid – work for yourself.

I remember accepting a client with various tax issues. I'm not a tax specialist and I'm mainly good at more general consulting. Nevertheless, I decided to work with that client. This caused me incredible headaches. I had to immerse myself in things I had no knowledge of and which I didn't like. I calculated later what I earned from this apparently well-paying client. I arrived at just a few dollars per hour. The many hours of unpaid research had cost me dearly. Our arrangement did not specify payment for my hours of research. If you decide to charge for research, you may have a dissatisfied client because the invoice would be many times higher than expected.

Choose a niche

This kind of situation can be avoided if you specialize, if you choose a niche. A niche is a specific target group or sector where you feel at home, where you speak the language, where you move easily, and where you can add value without spending too much energy. It is a place where you have a head start over the competition. If you work in a niche, it is much easier to attract clients. Accountants who sell everything to everyone get lost in the crowd. They don't distinguish themselves in any area and find clients thanks to word-of-mouth. Relying on referrals means that you have little influence on which clients you attract, and you have no clue whether any given client will be your ideal client. If you want to grow, you can start advertising, but if your advertising message focuses on "all entrepreneurs in the country," you will find it difficult to advertise in a targeted way and miss the opportunity to appeal to specific clients with specific needs.

If you start focusing on a niche, it affects three areas:

1. The more you know about your client's business, the more valuable you become and the higher your rate can be.

2. Having a niche distinguishes you from the "ordinary" accountant.

3. You make it easier for yourself. As soon as you choose one target group or industry, you will know your clients' problems before they do. You will know almost everything about the software being used and the tax rules.

In short: it will be easier to find clients and you can deliver much more value with far less effort.

Looking for the ideal client is a distressing step for most entrepreneurs. As soon as you start reducing the market from all potential clients to only the entrepreneurs from a specific sector or target group, you limit your market potential from a million to a few hundred thousand or even a few tens of thousands. This may feel counterintuitive, but this will make it a lot easier for you to attract clients and, to deliver extraordinary value to them without extraordinary effort.

Since the autumn of 2017, I have focused with Profit First Professionals on bookkeepers, accountants, and business coaches. Because I used to focus on solopreneurs, I'm working in a new niche and with a completely new target group. I felt a bit tense at first, but it paid off almost immediately. It was easier for me to get in touch with my ideal client, sales calls were almost effortless, and my clients achieved great results very quickly.

An additional effect was that I was soon asked to give interviews for trade journals, such as *Activa* (published by the Netherlands Association of Administration and Tax Experts or NOAB) and *AccountancyVanmorgen* (published by the National Network for Accountants). Being recognized as an expert in my niche has brought me even more ideal clients.

People want to work with the best!

As soon as you say that "all entrepreneurs" are your potential client, you are doing both yourself and the potential client a disservice. The moment you try to address "everyone", you really don't address anyone. People want to be helped by the best, but if you claim to be able to help everyone, you aren't the best at anything. If you specialize and become an expert in a sector or target group, you make it much easier for your client to choose you. It becomes easier for your clients to refer their colleagues to you: "Hey, you're a hairdresser, aren't you? Then you need to talk to John, who is a profit advisor to hairdressers. He knows everything about the profession, and I'm sure he can help you achieve your goals."

One of the Profit First Professionals trained by me, focuses mainly on the hospitality industry. That's a pretty specific industry. The fact that she knows everything about margins, supplier agreements, specific software, POS systems, common problems and pitfalls, means that clients find her and not the other way around. She's the preferred profit advisor for her industry.

Once you have chosen an area to specialize in, you can become smarter in that area every day. You will read trade journals, listen to podcasts, adjust your news feed. You learn daily, and that makes you increasingly valuable to your clients. Your clients will achieve great results by working with you and will recommend you to colleagues from the same industry. They will happily pay you more, because you help them earn more too.

Your client is easier to find if you know where to look

Finding new clients becomes a lot easier if you know exactly where to look. "Just placing an advertisement" is like firing buckshot. You have little control over exactly what you hit. Advertising in the trade magazine that your favorite client reads is significantly more effective. If you can closely target your Facebook ads, you'll get many more leads for the same investment. Visiting a trade fair is a very tiring activity – at least, I think so. Especially when you're constantly talking to someone you know right away will never become your client. But going to a fair where 80% of the visitors can become your client because they all fall into your niche, that's wonderful! And how about those clients who find you spontaneously, because they Google "accountant for physiotherapists" and immediately see your name on the first page. That is a great introduction! It immediately creates trust, because you appear to know what you are talking about.

Three other common concerns

I have already mentioned one major concern for entrepreneurs: that they will attract fewer clients if they specialize. There are more concerns:

1. Can you never work with other clients again?

Many entrepreneurs are afraid that they have to say "no" to all clients who are not their ideal client, that they not only miss out on clients, but also exclude people who need their help. Remember: You are the boss. You can take any client you want. Even if you focus on a specific target group, there is nothing to stop you from welcoming a client from another niche if you want to. You will make your own life a lot easier, however, if you declare your expertise to the outside world in your communication. Compare it to having a store and a warehouse. In the store window, you display what you want to sell the most, but you also store other products in the warehouse.

2. *Isn't it boring to specialize?*

Another widely expressed concern is that specializing is boring. Entrepreneurs love to be challenged all the time and to diversify constantly. "More of the same" may sound uninteresting, but just emphasize the first word: more. Within your specialization, you can increase and widen your knowledge. You can tackle any problem coming your way. Your client is dissatisfied with his software package? You know exactly which package suits her, because you know the five most important packages in the industry inside out. Your client wants to apply for funding? You can recommend three investors and you start working with him to prepare the application. Your client has a problem with margins? You see what goes wrong because you recently had a client with the same problem. Your client wants to open an extra division? You have experience in this complex process and you're ready to provide expert advice and support. The added value you can deliver is huge. And that means that you can quickly go beyond the boring "basic work" and really explore one industry in depth. You are rightly a profit advisor.

3. *Can I live up to expectations?*

As soon as you start positioning yourself as an expert, you will be noticed. The chance of getting media coverage suddenly increases. Others will start talking about you. You may feel some fear. The imposter syndrome may rear its head. Women, in particular, appear to suffer from feelings of inadequacy. Despite abundant proof of their competence (their clients are satisfied and achieve great results, they have many certificates on the wall and they are approached as experts by the media), people with this syndrome continue to feel that they are imposters and do not deserve their success. Proofs of success are not attributed to one's own competence, but dismissed as luck, good timing or major incompetence of others. As soon as you choose a specialization, you stand out from the crowd. It helps if you realize that you only need to know a little more than anyone else about a specific discipline or subject in order to be able to help clients in your targeted industry.

Identifying your ideal client

How do you find out who your ideal client is? Your ideal client may be in a specific industry or target group, but it can also be someone with a specific problem. Your ideal client is always someone you love to work with. Working with this entrepreneur can be effortless.

When I was still teaching "Finance for non-financial managers", my ideal clients were managers who really didn't know anything about finance. Some of them didn't even know the difference between a balance sheet and a profit and loss statement. As soon as I started to work with them, I became enthusiastic. In no time, I could give managers both confidence and new skills. If I was approached to give a follow-up training (a training to managers who already had a good financial basis), I consistently declined. They were not my ideal clients. I didn't enjoy working with them, but worse still, they often found my approach too simplistic. Because I knew my ideal client so well, I could easily make choices and I did my work effortlessly and with great pleasure.

Your ideal client is often already there; you just don't realize it. You only need to identify those clients and address them in your marketing message, so great prospects know how to find you.

Let's do a quick experiment.

Imagine that the doorbell rings. Your ideal client is at the door. Before you let him (or her) in, it is important that you create him exactly the way you want him to be! You don't have to make any concessions, nor do you have to worry that it will be final. Your ideal client may and will change, deepen or transform over the days, weeks, months, and years to come. Create your ideal client as you would like to help him right now. Who is there? Is it a man? A woman? Old? Young? What about his hobbies or interests? Does he own a large or a small business? Does he have any employees? What is the company's legal form? What is his revenue? Does he have a production company? Services? Trade? What kind of person is he? What are your ideal client's important values? How is he relating to you? How much does he pay you for your services? What is his biggest problem? Create the ideal picture and do not make any concessions. You don't have to wonder if your picture is realistic. It is your picture. You can make it the way you want. Does the image of this ideal client make you happy? How would it be to focus on this ideal client?

Perhaps this little experiment will give you the first idea of your ideal client. You may discover that he is in an industry in which you have a lot of experience, or in an industry in which you have hardly any experience, but which makes your heart beat faster. There are no good or bad choices; it's just a matter of experimenting, discovering and getting ever closer to your ideal client.

The Client Assessment

You can also discover who your ideal client is by looking at your current client base. A good exercise is the Client Assessment. See Figure 2.

CLIENT	SALES (YEAR)	HOURS (P/M)	$ PER HOUR	$ PER HOUR ☺☺☹	FINAN-CIAL ☺☺☹	COMMU-NICATION	VALUES	...	AVERAGE SCORE
Example client A	$15.000	10	$125	9	8	9	9		8,6
Example client B	$12.000	10	$100	8	7	8	8		7,6
Example client C	$12.000	15	$67	6	5	6	6		5,6

Figure 2: *Client Assessment* (inspired by the Assessment Chart from *The Pumpkin Plan* by Mike Michalowicz)

Step 1

Make an overview of all your clients of the past twelve months, and sort them by revenue from large to small. Put these clients with their revenue in an Excel spreadsheet and add some columns to it.

Hours

Next to the revenue column you add an Hour column. Here you note how many hours per month you spend on each client.

$ per hour

In the next column you calculate the average hourly rate by comparing the revenue amount with the number of hours you spend on the client.

$ per hour

To what extent does the rate match your wishes and requirements? You will need this column to assess the hourly rate (in step 2).

How happy does each client make you? Do you answer the phone when she calls? Or do you pretend you can't hear the phone? Do you look forward to a meeting with him? In the morning, do you like to start your day with her account?

Financial

Also look at your clients from the financial perspective. Does the client pay the bills on time? Is there room for growth in sales or has this client already reached maximum revenue?

Communication

How does communication go with each client? Do you get

quick responses to questions? Does each client ask clear questions? Do they respect your working hours? Do they do their "homework?"

Values

Does the client match the values you consider important?

Other

If necessary, add other criteria that are important to you when evaluating your client.

Step 2

Rate all clients on the various criteria. Give each client 5 points if they score very high on a criterion, o if it really can't get worse and 1, 2, 3, or 4 if it's in between.

Step 3

Calculate the average score per client. If you find a certain criterion very important, you can include it in your assessment double or triple.

Step 4

Now sort the overview by average score. Your most ideal client is at the top, while the least ideal client is at the bottom.

This assessment gives you a wealth of information. Not only do you get insight into your current client base, you also learn what kind of clients you want more of. Focus on those clients! Don't hesitate to talk to clients who score low in the assessment. You can adjust your rate or service package or, if nothing can be done to improve things, say goodbye to such a client. At www.theprofitadvisor.eu you can download a Client Assessment for free.

3.4 Which steps do you take to solve your client's problem?

Being clear about the problems and the real goals of your ideal client helps you in many ways. It makes it easier to acquire new clients, the sales conversation goes more smoothly, it gives the collaboration with the client a clear direction and it helps in determining your rates. But before you can sell and deliver these results, you must first translate the problems and goals of your ideal client into the products you are going to sell. As a profit advisor, you no longer sell hours. The client doesn't just want you to do stuff; the client expects results. You have already mapped the results of your ideal client. The next question that arises is: how does my client get from the current situation to the desired situation? What steps does he take in collaboration with me?

You may be tempted to say that there is no general answer, that this differs per client. And that is partly true: ultimately, the collaboration with each client will be different. But the broad lines can be determined. This is not only great for you, since you don't have to reinvent the wheel every time, but also for your clients. They know where they stand. They understand your expectations and timelines, and they know what you will deliver.

Again, compare this to building a house. Your home will be very different from that of your exercise buddy at the gym. I understand that. But the steps that you and your exercise buddy take on the way to your new house are broadly the same. I don't know much about building houses, but in general it will look something like this:

- *Step 1: Dreams.* What are your wishes and dreams? What does your new house look like in your mind?

- *Step 2: Architect.* Have an architect draw the plans that visualize your dream.
- *Step 3: Plot of land.* Look for a plot of land on which your dream home can be built.
- *Step 4: Money.* Make sure that you get the funding.
- *Step 5: Contractor.* Call in a contractor.

You can make the same step-by-step plan for the path your ideal client takes to solve his problem or problems.

By way of example, let me tell you what steps I take with entrepreneurs. My ideal client is you. I mainly work with bookkeepers, accountants and business coaches. But my ideal clients used to be solopreneurs who generated sales between $250,000 and $1,000,000. They worked with an old-school accountant. They paid this accountant too much and didn't really understand their finances. They had successful companies with increasing sales, but profits weren't increasing. I used to go through three steps in a twelve-month process with these clients:

- *Step 1: The basics in order.* This step usually took four to six months. We moved the accounting completely online, and we worked on new accounting processes and habits. Sometimes it was necessary to switch to a new accountant. These were often difficult months, when the skeletons came out of the closet and bitter pills had to be swallowed.
- *Step 2: The profitable plan.* Once we knew what the financial position of the entrepreneur was thanks to real-time information, we started to work on the profitable plan. We translated goals into figures, so that we knew if plans were feasible and where the focus should be.
- *Step 3: Steering with Profit First.* The third step was to

set up Profit First, so that the entrepreneur could make daily choices just by looking at bank accounts. Our intention was to have enough money to pay the tax bill, set aside profit first and never spend more than they should.

In the following chapters I will discuss these three parts in more detail, because they can help you better advise your client. Before I do that, we should look at the steps your ideal clients go through when they start to work with you.

Which steps does your client go through?

Which three to ten steps does your client go through to achieve his goals? Take the time to think about your ideal client's journey. Set aside a strategy day. Determine the steps and write them down for yourself. You will refine and adapt them over time, but these steps form the basis of your program, of your unique way of helping your clients achieve their goals.

As soon as you have your program set up, you can start testing it on a trial client. This is a win-win situation. You get the opportunity to develop and fine-tune your unique program, and your client will achieve results for an investment that – in this phase – is a lot less than what you will ask for later.

Once you have refined your unique step-by-step plan, you will have something tangible in your hands. You no longer sell time, you sell results. These results are much more marketable than the dime-a-dozen "I'm an accountant" sales pitches. Last but not least – a unique program that helps achieve visible results can eventually become independent of you. You can have parts of your program run by others, so that your company will generate money even when you don't work yourself.

3.5 At what price do you market your services?

Being paid by the hour is not only an unattractive earning model for you, it is also unattractive for your client. For you, being paid on an hourly basis means that you can only earn more if you work more hours, if your price per hour goes up or if you let others work for you. Moreover, you are not an hour-factory. You are an advisor with a wealth of knowledge and experience. Sometimes asking the right question can generate thousands of dollars for the client. Being paid for the value you deliver is therefore much more logical and satisfying.

It's also unappealing for your client to pay you by the hour. The client doesn't want hours; the client wants a solution for a problem and prefers to acquire that solution as efficiently as possible. Once you start working on an hourly basis, friction can arise over the number of hours needed to deliver a solution. Worse still, sometimes a lot of time has been invested and the client doesn't even have a solution for his problem. It is therefore much more logical to determine the rate based on the value that you deliver, rather than the hours you spend. How do you determine the value of the solutions you deliver?

Manage your own mindset

If you're going to sell results instead of hours, the biggest step is managing your own thoughts. In my experience, this is a process. You can't do anything if you don't see the value of your own services. It helps enormously if you begin to see that your clients earn significantly more through your advice. When I saw that my clients were earning tens of thousands of euros a year thanks to our collaboration, I was very happy and proud on the one hand, but on the other hand something started to pinch. I had not yet earned a fraction of what working with me had brought them. The value I delivered was not commensurate to the monetary reward I had received. It was not a win-win at all, just a win for my clients.

Recognizing the value you deliver is essential. But that is not all. We are so used to calculating everything back to an hourly rate that at first it is quite difficult to determine the value of your service. This too is a process. Allow yourself time to ask yourself again and again: what does this mean for the client? And, certainly, don't hesitate to ask the client: "If you look back now, what has the process we have been through over the past few months brought you?"

Determine the cost of the problem

Determine what the problem costs. This gives you an indication of the value of your solution. If Robert spends one day a month putting his prehistoric accounting in order, and his own hourly rate is 100 dollars, then the cost of that problem is already 800 dollars per month. But I'm sure Robert has even more problems. If his margins are abominable, that problem easily costs him hundreds, thousands or tens of thousands of dollars per month. If he lies awake at night because of financial worries, it is difficult to express these costs in dollars, but you can include them when determining your value. Worries reduce the entrepreneur's creativity and effectiveness and, therefore, worries cost money.

Determine the intrinsic value of your program or service

If you have developed a unique program that is proven to help your clients solve their problems and achieve their goals, this program represents a value in itself. Thanks to your wisdom, years of experience and creative power, you were able to design a unique solution to a problem your ideal client faces. This solution consists of a step-by-step plan, a process or template that can be used time and again. In fact, you don't have to go through that program or process with your client personally. Your team can do that for you too. But because you have developed a unique and proven program, clients pay significantly more than your team members' hourly rate would justify. They get more than hours; they get a proven solution.

New clients

It is often not that difficult to present your new price structure to new clients. If, during the sales conversation (see Chapter 7), you clearly understand the client's pain, and the solution you offer is visibly more valuable than the investment in that solution, then the client will easily say "yes" to your offer.

Current clients

With current clients, you'll probably want to switch from your current price structure to your new one. That can be more difficult. As soon as you ask Robert, for example, to pay more for the same thing, you at least owe him an explanation. The best thing, of course, would be to show him that the new situation is also a "win" for him and delivers him significantly more value. You talk to Robert about his situation and tell him how you think you can serve him even better. Then you explain that you only work according to the new structure starting from a given date. You ask your client to switch to your new model, giving him enough time to make a choice. If your client does not want any added value (say Robert just wants to file the tax returns as cheaply as possible), you give him the opportunity to look for another service provider. He may decide to leave. If you are not okay with that, you shouldn't take this step... at least not yet. At the same time, it is very likely that the client will be very happy with your new offer. He may even have been waiting for it!

Action step

This chapter was effectively one big action step:

- Determine who your ideal client is.
- Look for your client's real problems and formulate the real solution.
- Design a step-by-step plan that you will go through time and again to solve the problems of your ideal client.
- Determine the value of your solution.

In this chapter, we discussed how you are going to solve the problem of your ideal client and the value of that solution. The following chapters discuss the steps I have taken with thousands of clients (from self-employed entrepreneurs to SMEs) in recent years. These steps have proven to be effective time and again and I expect that they will inspire you to determine your own ideal solution.

---

1. Source: Report by Central Bureau of Statistics Netherlands (CBS): "Armoede en sociale uitsluiting 2018" ("Poverty and social exclusion, 2018;" no English translation available). A 2015 study by Slivinski among low-income Americans show that there is more poverty (0,38%) amongst entrepreneurs compared with the general population (0,3%) (https://books.google.nl/books?id=T-x6DwAAQBAJ&pg=PT57&lpg=PT57&dq=poverty+rates+entrepreneurs&source=bl&ots=zXGvFMuK64&sig=ACfU3U3rZ_JhZHmsGDAKdp56yiEooEzImQ&hl=en&sa=X&ved=2ahUKEwiKgNaN7-7mAhXFCOwKHYyWASYQ6AEwDHoECAwQAQ#v=onepage&q=poverty%20rates%20entrepreneurs&f=false)

4 ADMINISTRATION IN 30 MINUTES PER WEEK PLUS ONE MINUTE PER DAY

* * *

We are what we repeatedly do. Excellence, therefore, is not an act but a habit – Will Durant

* * *

Peter and I got a lukewarm welcome. If your client hires an advisor, and that advisor wants to meet with you as an accountant, you know that something is wrong. We were offered coffee as a weak attempt to appear polite. Meanwhile I let my eyes wander around the office. It was an old-fashioned office: wall-to-wall carpeting, blinds. There were piles of paper everywhere. There were four large steel file cabinets, which I suspected were packed with file folders. This place confirmed my earlier suspicions. I was not dealing with a modern accountant. This was not an accountant who works in the cloud and embraces digital developments. This was a typical old-fashioned accountant.

After the obligatory small talk, I asked an important, and what I thought to be innocent question. "I understand that last year's figures are not yet complete," I started, "but I'm curious about Peter's provisional figures. What are they in terms of revenue and profit?"

Greg looked surprised. He couldn't give me this information. There were no provisional figures.

I was confused. "You have filed the sales tax returns, haven't you?" I tried. "Then there must be provisional figures, right?"

Greg's answer stunned me. "We did the sales tax return manually, in Excel. We have not yet entered anything in the accounting software."

That's what he said.

I fell silent. I had seen a lot in the processes I went through with my clients, but this just took the cake.

* * *

Now that you have an idea of your ideal clients and their real problems and goals, we dive deeper into the content. What do you as a profit advisor provide that a regular accountant does not? How do you add so much value that you can call yourself a profit advisor?

On the one hand, the answer, of course, depends on your expertise and skills. On the other hand, there are several steps that almost every entrepreneur must take. I'll walk you through them in this and the following chapter!

Step 1: You help your clients do their bookkeeping in 30 minutes per week (this chapter).

Step 2: You support your client in making a profit plan (Chapter 5).

Step 3: You teach your client how to manage finances with the help of Profit First (Chapter 6).

Before you can really help the client to make more profit, to build the fun parts of the house, the foundation must be in order. Accounting must be accurate before you can start on the stuff you dream of: building that beautiful kitchen or, in entrepreneurial terms, making a profit. The accounts must be in order every day with as little time, energy and money as possible.

In this chapter, I will show you why bookkeeping costs too much and explain how to guide clients step by step, so they can do their bookkeeping in 30 minutes per week.

4.1 The agony of doing the administration

Ask entrepreneurs how their accounts are doing, and they'll ask if you can suggest a more fun subject. I gave a lot of webinars to entrepreneurs, and I always asked several questions via a poll. One of these questions was:

"What does accounting cost you?"

a. Too much time
b. Too much money
c. Too much energy
d. Too much time, money and energy
e. I am very satisfied with my bookkeeping

An average webinar produced the following results (see Figure 3).

We can cautiously conclude that two-thirds of entrepreneurs are not happy with their finances. Bookkeeping takes too much time, too much money, too much energy or all of the above! Not surprisingly, they prefer to talk about something else.

I am very satisfied with my bookkeeping 34%
Too much time 17%
Too much money 12%
Too much (negative) energy 26%
Too much time, money and energy 11%

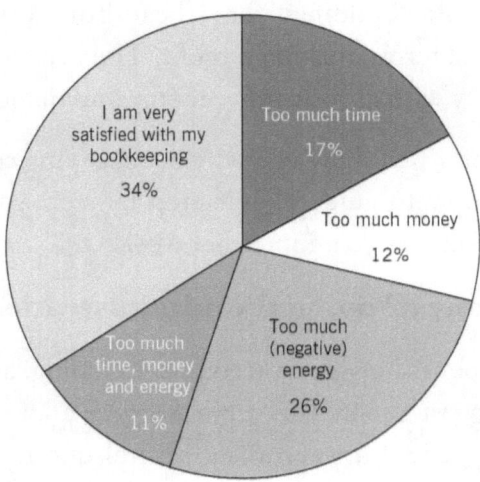

Figure 3: *Answers to the question: "What does accounting cost you?"*

Check your Facebook or Twitter timeline the day before the deadline of the sales tax return and filter on "sales tax". Without exception, you will see messages such as:

Entrepreneurial suffering summarized in 2 short words: #salestax

Unbelievable sh*t weather, so it's time for the quarterly f*ing job: the sales tax return!
#hopefullyfinishedquicklythistime #salestax #return

Meh... #administration #return, hassle with #receipts, #bookkeeping and #salestax also part of it...

so, the once a quarter stressor is out of the door again: #salestax #return filed again!

Why is it that filing the sales tax return is such a drama for entrepreneurs? One of the biggest problems is that entrepreneurs bury their heads in the sand for three months and do their best to ignore bookkeeping. And then, if they really can't postpone anymore, sometimes literally at ten minutes before the filing deadline, the chaos that has been accumulating over three months must be cleared up. It is no surprise that this leads to stress and aversion.

The solution is as simple as it is complex. The client needs accounting habits, processes and systems. If accounting is a daily habit, it hardly requires time and energy and is always up to date. Compare it to brushing your teeth. Most people don't really like brushing their teeth. And yet we all brush our teeth twice a day. This is a fascinating phenomenon, because why do we do something when we don't feel like it? There are at least two main reasons for this:

1. It is a habit. We are taught to do so from an early age. You brush your teeth twice a day for two minutes at a time. It's that simple.

2. The consequences of stopping this habit are disastrous. If you only brush your teeth once a year or once a quarter, you'll soon

have to go for root canal treatments or even dentures. And nobody wants that.

It is exactly for these two reasons that you must make accounting a habit:

1. When the bookkeeping is updated daily, your clients never again have to ask themselves if they're in the mood for bookkeeping. They just do it.

2. The consequences of quarterly accounting are disastrous. Compared to daily updates, it can take up to ten times as long to update the accounts once every quarter. Lost receipts, reminders that you have to send your client time after time, receipts that remain lost even after you have reminded them several times, transactions that nobody really understands anymore, even after looking at them for an hour – it all costs a lot of money. Literally thousands of dollars are wasted annually because accounting is not a habit but an activity that gets postponed for weeks or months.

Imagine what life would be like if all your clients spent one minute a day on their accounts, as a daily habit? All receipts and invoices are sent into the system straightaway. You will never have to chase receipts again. Receipt will no longer get lost. Imagine what that would mean for your internal processes and procedures. The work is much easier to organize, because you do just a little every day, instead of a mountain of work once a quarter. Your team won't be playing ping-pong all summer, whereas in April they need to work night shifts.

And that's just the internal processes. Imagine what it would mean for your clients if they could submit their sales tax returns at the end of the quarter without any stress and effort, with a simple push of a button. And what it would mean for your clients who can see how they're doing financially with just a glance at a dashboard because their bookkeeping is updated regularly. And what it would mean for the results if you could help your clients make more profit thanks to this foundation. Once this is all in place, it is heaven. However, depending on the client's starting position, laying this foundation can take some effort.

It is your task to guide your client in implementing the processes and habits of handling accounting in one minute per day and 30 minutes per week. I'll give you the three basic requirements and the seven steps to achieve this.

4.2 Administration in 30 minutes per week

Before your client can manage all the bookkeeping in one minute a day plus 30 minutes a week, three basic requirements must be met:

1. The bookkeeping must be done entirely online.

2. Full use must be made of technological developments.

3. The processes must be established, organized and consistently implemented.

Basic requirement 1: Ensure online accounting

Your clients may say they're not interested. Or maybe you've been an accountant for fifteen years and you're still doing things the old-fashioned way. But for you as a profit advisor, offline bookkeeping is no longer a realistic option for two reasons:

1. You need your client to deliver receipts and invoices, and you want that delivery to be as smooth and as fast as possible, so you can put your effort into helping your client generate more profit. You don't want to lose any receipts, you don't want to have to remind the client of the receipts that still have to be submitted,

and you certainly don't want your internal processes to be dictated by the client.

2. You and your client both need real-time insight into figures, not last year's and not even last quarter's. Not even via a report that you draw up and send once a month. Account activity through the previous day must be available and current so that the client can check the books while waiting for the train. Simply put, all your clients need to be online.

Basic requirement 2: Use technological developments

In addition to the online accounting software, there are many other technological developments that help you and your client save time, money and energy. They may take some time to research and install, but once operational, you save time and increase profits for everyone. I'm referring to automatic links with banks, linking the shopping cart with the accounting system, scanning and recognition functions, invoicing from the accounting system (and not from Word, Excel or anotherinvoicingsystem.com that is not linked to the accounting package), the use of RCSFI and UBL, among others. And there is much more to come in the near future. Lead the way, save your client the trouble and let computers do the work.

Basic requirement 3: Set up processes

This point perhaps costs the most if it's not in order. And, unfortunately, almost all entrepreneurs lag a bit behind in this area. Often the most basic processes are not set up correctly and therefore lead to high costs, for example, mixing up private and business expenses and not filing receipts and invoices in an organized manner. But it's also about the slightly more complex processes: how do you get the revenue from your shopping cart system into the accounting program? Often, entrepreneurs just cobble a solution together, and that can end up costing a lot of money.

My favorite example is the ten-dollar pizza... which ultimately costs more than fifty dollars.

Suppose your client – let's call him Omar – works late with his team and orders pizzas. The pizzas are delivered, he takes the receipt for $44.95 from the top pizza box and puts it on his desk (action 1). The team feasts on the pizzas. The next day, when processing the bank statement, you see an expense of $44.95, which is not matched by a receipt. You book the amount on the suspense account for unclassified transactions (action 2). At the end of the month, you send the list with unclassified transactions to Omar (action 3). He receives the mail in his inbox, looks at it and doesn't feel like doing anything about it (action 4). In the following days, he will look ten times at the email that he still doesn't want to act upon (actions 5 through 14). You send him a reminder email (action 15). Omar decides to take action and starts looking for the receipt. He turns his entire desk upside down but can't find the receipt (action 16). At the end of the day he makes another attempt and he finally finds the receipt (action 17). He sends you the receipt with a short explanation (action 18). You receive the email (action 19), but you are working with another client and do nothing with it. The next day you look at Omar's email. You open his accounting software and process the receipt (action 20). When you add up all the time spent on one little expense, the pizzas for $44.95 now cost $244.95.

Is this a cynical story? Yes, somewhat. Is it exaggerated? No, not really. You know as well as I do that troubleshooting and chasing receipts is by far the largest inefficiency in your client's accounting. That costs the client thousands of dollars per year in actions that you, by the way, would much rather not have to do. Just imagine what it would mean if you never again saw unclassified transactions on the suspense account, because Omar and your other clients always scan or email receipts directly into the accounting software. You will both notice the effect of the increased efficiency in your wallets. Of course, your clients will also benefit from the fact that you spend less time on their accounting. And, at the same time, they will happily pay you a higher rate than they would pay an old-school bookkeeper who doesn't help him with efficient processes. You've identified Omar's biggest annoyance; help him get rid of it.

4.3 Accounting in 30 minutes per week

The first challenge is to help your clients do their bookkeeping as if they were brushing their teeth. It's not one miserable long haul at the end of a quarter, but a daily habit. Once accounting has become a habit, they no longer have to think about whether they feel like doing their admin. They just do it. A second challenge is to work according to the First Time Right principle (from Lean Six Sigma). This is aimed at ensuring that as many actions as possible are done right the first time. Making a mistake, discovering it and then correcting it is always more expensive than doing it right the first time. Moreover, it also annoys the client.

With the three basic requirements – online accounting, making use of technological developments and setting up the processes – clearly in our sights, we can look at the step-by-step plan that guides an entrepreneur to do the accounting in 30 minutes per week plus one minute per day. Share this step-by-step plan with your client. Clients know where they stand, and – not unimportantly – also immediately understand why the investment may be higher than what they would pay the accountant around the corner. They immediately and deeply understand the value of your services.

Step 1: Online bookkeeping

Provide an entrepreneur-friendly online accounting system. Your clients can email purchase invoices to such a system and can create sales invoices as well. They can also scan receipts directly into the accompanying app. Preferably choose software that links with your client's bank, so that transactions will be automatically entered into the accounting software on a daily basis. Of course, you also need a login option, so that you can perform all the actions necessary to comply with accounting and tax obligations.

One important choice you need to make is whether you want to have one standard system that all your clients will work with, or whether you and your client will select from a number of options, which means that you and your team will have to work with several systems. Having one fixed system for all your clients has countless advantages. You and your team only need to master one system. You only need to find out once what links with other applications need to be created. You reduce costs through economy of scale. If you have a very straightforward ideal client, this may also have advantages for your business. You have chosen the package that best suits the industry, so you can advise clients without having to examine several systems for each one. On the other hand, working with a fixed system may limit you. What if your ideal client knocks on the door, and is happy working with software that is not your preferred one? What do you do then?

You must think about this in advance. In Chapter 11, I will discuss the choice of the right software in more detail.

Step 2: Linking and setting up systems

Reserve enough time to link the various systems your client works with (accounting, shopping cart, bank, cash register system, etc.) and set them up properly. You need the client to set up the systems. Discuss together what insight the client needs in both revenue and expenses and create new accounts in the chart of accounts, with terms that are useful to your client. I still see accounts with names that don't have any meaning for the client. It is useful, however, to have a clear account per product. The client then discovers, for example, that a particular time-consuming product yields almost nothing. Also discuss with the client which cost categories are important to keep an eye on, and make sure those costs have their own account name.

Also discuss how to create the sales invoice. Working with products that are linked correctly to the chart of accounts saves the client a lot of time when invoicing and helps avoid mistakes.

Depending on the software, there are many ways to save time and money and to provide insight into figures. This way you help make finances fun, practical and accessible for your client, and that quickly makes you a highly valued advisor!

Step 3: Division of tasks

Make clear arrangements about who does what and when. First, focus on the main issues. An important question is who processes the purchase invoices? Does the client do it personally, or do you handle it? In my experience, there are pros and cons to both options.

When clients process their own invoices, it prevents frustration on their part. "No, that doesn't go there!" or "How can these costs be so low? I missed an invoice!" However, the client is more likely than you are to make mistakes. For example, how does he deal with foreign invoices? You will have to check them afterwards. There are, of course, other ways to organize your collaboration. Many clients just don't want to do it themselves. In that case, it is important to go through the chart of accounts together in detail, so that there will be a chart of accounts that will provide insight (see also step 2 about setting up the system) and you will also know precisely what needs to be recorded on which account.

Processing the bank statement is usually left to you. However, there are also many clients who prefer to do it themselves, because they like to stay in control or because they still don't earn enough to outsource it. The same applies to filing the sales tax return. This is often a task for the accountant, who then immediately checks the figures. Filing a sales tax return, especially in the first three quarters of the year, is effectively just a matter of pressing a button. Business owners can typically manage that themselves. In my experience, there is no single right way, as long as you agree very clearly which way you are going and you both stick to it.

Write down this task division so that you have a document to fall back on. You can do that on one page. Especially in the beginning you will have to educate your clients. It takes a while before the new behavior becomes a habit. During those weeks you want to be able to point out their tasks to them. It helps if you can fall back on a document where the arrangements are clearly written down.

Step 4: Setting up processes

In addition to the software, new processes must also be set up. You can possibly achieve the greatest savings here! Most likely, you've been annoyed countless times by the way your clients submit accounts or how they do book keeping. The first three times you wonder why, for example, one client consistently uses the wrong account. But the correction only takes you a few mouse clicks. After a while, you get used to it. A new status quo is born – one that costs a lot of money in the long run. You can prevent this waste of resources by going through the processes together. Give feedback as soon as they deviate from the arrangements or make mistakes. The processes include:

1. Receiving purchase invoices

2. Processing purchase invoices

3. Receiving and processing receipts

4. Sending sales invoices

5. Paying purchase invoices

6. Credit management

However, depending on your client, there are even more processes conceivable, such as inventory management, cash payments, etc.

1. Receiving purchase invoices

What do your clients do when they receive a purchase invoice by email? It is very likely that they don't do anything. Many entrepreneurs leave purchase invoices in their Inbox because they have never thought about the way to process them quickly and efficiently. That costs money. You know that, and I know that. All you need to do is help your clients set up a transparent and easy process. There isn't just one right process. It's vital that whatever process you develop should be so easy and logical that the clients can do it over and over again, until it becomes a habit. Having one fixed sequence of steps prevents the invoice from being lost, paid twice or handled fifteen times before being taken care of. I share a standard process with you, but of course that doesn't have to be the ideal process for your clients.

Example process (accounting software with payment function):

1. Email the invoice to your accounting package immediately upon receipt.

2. Create a payment run on a fixed day of the week (explanation under point 5, Paying purchase invoices, below) and pay the invoices.

Example process (simple accounting software):

1. Email the invoice to your accounting software immediately upon receipt.

2. Then drag the invoice to the "Invoice to be paid" folder.

3. Pay all invoices from the "Invoices to be paid" folder on a fixed day of the week (explanation under point 5, Paying purchase invoices, below).

Believe it or not, some purchase invoices are sent by the old-fashioned post office. They get lost even more often than digital invoices; they get pushed around on the desk or end up somewhere in a drawer. The following also applies to these invoices: set up a fixed process. I always take a picture of the purchase invoice and email it to myself immediately. It then goes through the same process as a digital purchase invoice. But you can, of course, also think of other processes. It is important that your client should always follow the same steps in the same order.

2. *Processing purchase invoices*

When processing purchase invoices, the First Time Right principle is extremely important. A purchase invoice recorded on the wrong account initially causes a lot of irritation for the client. The entrepreneur must then either correct the error or ask you to do so. The first option is often faster, but with the second option there is a greater chance that you will process a similar invoice properly the next time. In any case, booking an invoice right the first time takes less time than making a mistake first, then discovering it and finally correcting it.

A second important point of attention when processing purchase invoices is the description that is given to the invoice. Many purchase invoices barely get a description, at best a single word like "rent" and at worst the standard description offered by the accounting software, which is for example identical to the name of the document. That almost always gives too little information. of course, you have no problem when you record an expense, but it becomes a big problem when you analyze the figures a few months later. Entrepreneurs who try to understand what they spent so much money on would benefit from clear descriptions. I recommend the following description for each line in the journal entry: what, who, when. For example: Phone bill, Verizon, Dec 20xx.

3. Receiving and processing receipts

Receipts are by far the biggest problem. They disappear into a wallet or handbag, never to be seen again. Receipts can cost a lot of time, energy and money. Sales tax cannot be claimed back; costs cannot be claimed. Clients really hate bookkeeping when they have to look for lost receipts. The solution is very simple: if your clients buy something and don't have any petty cash, make sure they pay by card. At the very least, you will prevent transactions from going missing. Then teach your clients to immediately scan the receipt – and by that I really mean immediately, while they are still in the store – with their bookkeeping app. Then they may throw away the receipt. If you can achieve this, you will have scored a major victory!

4. Sending sales invoices

Sending out sales invoices usually goes fine. Since this is the activity that brings in money, the entrepreneur usually masters this pretty quickly. Yet, by discussing the process step by step, you almost always discover that efficiency can be improved further. I know a lot of entrepreneurs who manually retype invoices that are automatically created by their shopping cart system. Instead of retyping the invoice, it's often possible to automate the process. If that is not an option, it might be possible to export and import monthly overviews. With some research, lots of time and energy can be saved in the process. Even when an entrepreneur creates invoices manually, much of it can be automated: from creating products (including price) in the accounting software and linking a time registration to working with a shopping cart that takes care of the entire invoicing. There are many possibilities.

Also look at the actual moment when the invoices are created. I often advise clients to do this much more frequently than once a month, for example once a week on the weekly admin day or twice a month. The longer your clients wait on invoicing, the longer it will take to get their money. For many entrepreneurs it can also be an eye-opener that they can send their invoice in advance and thus get paid in advance.

5. Paying purchase invoices

My first tip regarding payments is to discuss a fixed payment day. Many entrepreneurs pay their bills when they arrive. That is simply not efficient; they spend an unnecessary amount of time paying bills. In fact, if they've set up the process well in step 1, it is not necessary at all.

What can also be useful is to provide the payment with a fixed description. First, state the invoice number (and, if applicable, the purchase order number or any other required information), so the receiving party can process the payment. But add something more: what, who, when (for example: Telephone subscription Verizon January). Strictly speaking, it is not necessary, but entrepreneurs look at the bank more often than you think, especially if they work with Profit First (see Chapter 6). It is very useful for the entrepreneur if there is some information in the payment entry.

If the accounting software can run payment batches, make sure the entrepreneur uses that function!

It is generally a great relief to your clients that nothing else needs to be done! There is no need to write on the invoice that it has been paid; the invoice does not need to be stapled in alphabetical order in a folder or to the account statement. After it has been paid and emailed to the accounting program, it is ready.

6. *Credit management*

Reminding clients to pay unpaid invoices can be done in half a minute a week. This of course requires that certain conditions are in order: the accounting is done fully online, the software has the functionality to send reminders, the books are always up-to-date and standard texts have been created for reminders. If all that is set up, it is often a matter of one click and the reminder is sent.

The only thing that may stop your client from managing his debtors is his mindset. Strangely enough, many entrepreneurs find it difficult to send reminders. They are afraid they will be seen as bothersome or that they will lose clients. And that's why they don't do anything. But this non-paying client does cost them energy every day. Such entrepreneurs would definitely benefit if you helped them look at the credit management process from a business perspective. They may not realize that invoices can get lost and that some large companies only pay after the first reminder. A friendly reminder may then be enough to proceed to payment. But even if there is another reason, there is, of course, a contract. If the entrepreneur has kept to his side of the contract, it is only logical and appropriate that clients should be reminded to keep to their side of the contract. Help your clients set up this process and help them make sure they receive their money in a businesslike manner. That way, you will save your client a lot of frustration, time and money.

Would you like to receive this step-by-step plan in the form of a handy checklist? Download it for free at theprofitadvisor.eu.

4.4 Accounting habits

The promise in this chapter is that your clients can do their accounting in 30 minutes per week plus one minute per day. If your client is a huge multinational, that may not be a viable option, but for many solopreneurs and, in modified form, small SMEs, it really can be that easy. Of course, the three basic requirements in section 4.2 are in order, the step-by-step plan in section 4.3 has been completed and now your client must learn new accounting habits.

That last point can be a big challenge. We understand that most entrepreneurs have no natural interest in finance. They're often quite happy when they don't hear from you and when they don't need to do anything with accounting for weeks or months. But in the end, the bookkeeping is always there. Putting off admin chores doesn't make them go away. They always pile up.

I compared it to brushing your teeth and mentioned two important things:

1. When the bookkeeping is updated daily, your clients never again have to think about whether they're in the mood for doing the books. They just do it. Just like we don't question whether we feel like brushing our teeth. We just brush 'em.

2. The consequences of quarterly accounting are disastrous. Compared to daily updates, it can take up to ten times as long to update the accounts once every quarter. Just like the consequences of brushing your teeth once a month are disastrous. Before you know it, you need to undergo a root canal treatment.

From this point of view, it is not such a crazy idea to make a habit out of accounting. What does book keeping in 30 minutes per week plus one minute per day actually consist of?

One minute per day

Several activities must become ingrained as a daily habit. In order to help your clients, you give them regular feedback, especially during the first weeks. Praise them when you see that things are going well for days on end, but don't hesitate to immediately react if you're missing a receipt! Do not hesitate to appear "annoying". If you skip giving feedback in this phase, you'll find yourself back at square one and all the effort has been for nothing.

The daily activities may vary from person to person, but these activities are common:

- Scan receipts immediately upon receipt with an accounting app.
- Forward invoices that are received by email immediately to the accounting software and, if necessary, drag them to the folder "Invoices to be paid."
- Keep an eye on the bank accounts to get an idea of the cash flow.

30 minutes per week

On a fixed day, a fixed time even, the entrepreneur spends 30 minutes on his accounting. This includes:

- Profit First actions (see Chapter 6)
- Processing purchase invoices
- Creating sales invoices
- Sending reminders
- Paying purchase invoices
- Time and mileage recording

The introduction of the new systems, processes and habits will probably take several months. Once this has been achieved, it is important to reflect on this memorable moment and remind your clients of how far they've come. The entrepreneur is now ready for step 2: the profit plan!

Action step

Describe, as part of your unique program, which steps you go through with your ideal clients so they can manage the books in one minute per day and 30 minutes per week. Document this step-by-step plan. You now have a valuable product in your hands: a product that brings in money for both you and your client and helps you run your business efficiently.

Now that the basics are in place and the books are always in order without taking too much time, money and energy, the real work can begin. You are going to help the entrepreneur make a profit. There is a beautiful saying: "A goal without a plan is just a wish." In other words, achieving a good result first of all requires a solid plan. This is the subject of the following chapter: The Profit Plan.

5 SUPPORT YOUR CLIENT IN MAKING A PROFITABLE PLAN

* * *

A good result starts with a good plan – Femke Hogema

* * *

It soon became clear to me that in this first interview with Greg we would not get any insight into the finances of Peter's company. But I didn't want to return home empty-handed and hoped to get an idea of the financial situation by a different route. I spoke to Peter, but also counted on Greg's input.

"Peter," I started, "how do you earn your money?"

Peter looked at me, puzzled. "I sell apps," he said, cautiously.

"Great," I continued. "How many apps do you need to sell this year to achieve your profit target?" Now I had Peter's attention.

"Good question," he said. "I just don't have a good answer. If I knew that, it would be easier to manage my salesperson and put my schedule in order."

"What is your average margin on apps, Peter?" I asked, with a sidelong glance at Greg. "By that, I mean after you subtract the costs from your development team, what percentage is left?"

I looked at Peter, then at Greg, then at Peter again, waiting for an answer. I expected that one of them would be able to tell me how money was being made in this company.

* * *

Once the foundation is solid – the books are in order 24/7 with the least possible effort and costs – the best and most valuable work can start, that is, helping the client make a profit. Let me be absolutely clear, I do not mean theoretical, on-paper profit. I mean real money, the money you have in your hands. One of the most pioneering tools for this is the profitable plan.[1] A profitable plan is the translation of the entrepreneur's goals into figures: sales, costs and profit. A profitable plan shows whether businesses make a profit; whether they actually earn money.

It has some similarities with a budget. But the term "profitable plan" has a much greater appeal to business people, so that's the first hurdle out of the way. Other objections to more traditional budgets are that they can be cumbersome and feel theoretical. The profitable plan amply meets these concerns.

5.1 The objectives of the profitable plan

The profit plan has three main objectives:

1. Your clients know in advance whether their plans are feasible and whether they can earn enough with their dream, plan or idea.

2. It gives your clients focus and profit. They know what to do to create desired results.

3. The client can intervene and adjust in time if the desired results are not achieved.

Feasibility

It sounds obvious: entrepreneurs must determine in advance whether their plans are even feasible. But in my work with thousands of entrepreneurs over more than ten years, time and again it has turned out that this isn't obvious. Very few entrepreneurs determine in advance whether their plans are financially feasible. Generally, they spend a lot of time on the creative side of the idea. Entrepreneurs do everything in their power to elaborate plans in terms of content and to position themselves in the market. If you ask how much money they're going to make, they usually don't have an answer. Sometimes clients literally tell me: "As long as I do what I am good at, the money will follow."

Passion and perseverance are very powerful drivers. With them, an entrepreneur creates something out of nothing. But profit requires more than just passion. In reality, few entrepreneurs think through what the right price should be, what the cost price is, what the overhead costs are, and how much should be sold to be in the black. Entrepreneurs don't like to go there. Finances can be complex, and they don't know where to start. Working together with your clients to get a clear idea of how much they should actually sell and at what price is both powerful and essential. That's how goals are accomplished.

Focus and profit

A plan gives focus. Without a plan, some entrepreneurs fall into the trap of working from their mailbox and social media. As soon as they open their laptops in the morning, the work starts coming in. Everybody wants something: advice, an answer, a quote for a new project

There's always plenty to do when you're connected to the Internet. Sometimes an entrepreneur even earns a little money. A quote can result in an assignment, a coffee meeting can lead to a project. But beware, all these activities are driven by somebody else's need. Entrepreneurs without plans work reactively. They respond to what others want, which makes us question whether these reactive entrepreneurs are really doing what they want to do. Are they achieving their goals? Are they pursuing their dreams? Or, and this happens all too frequently, realizing at the end of the year that they indeed did make some money, but certainly didn't change the world.

When entrepreneurs work from a plan, they have focus. They know exactly what they must do this year, this month, this week, today, now, to make their dreams come true. They start working toward their own goals instead of reacting to the needs of others. They will also almost immediately make more profit, simply by doing the right things.

Managing

Having a plan also provides opportunities to work toward results. Since the books are in order, your clients can see, day by day, what they're selling and how much they're earning. As soon as they notice that their sales aren't what they want them to be or that they're not making the profit they want to make, the profit plan can show where things are going wrong. Perhaps the plan wasn't realistic. Great, that's a wake-up call. Sometimes clients must take action or accept that they won't achieve their goals. It's that simple. It may also be that their plan isn't entirely in line with what they really want. Fine, then they can adjust plans accordingly. Whatever the case, the combination of a plan and accurate figures give us valuable information.

Resistance to making a profit plan

Many entrepreneurs are reluctant to make a profit plan. They say, for example:

> *"I don't know how much I'm going to sell next year, do I?"*

"No," I always answer. "You don't know in advance how many clients you will attract and how much you will sell to them. But that's not the objective of the profit plan. The objective is that you should calculate in advance whether you can earn enough if you are going to do what you have in mind. If you can't make a profit on paper, you can't do it in real life either." It is also important that the entrepreneur understands that the profit plan is not carved in stone. It may be constantly changing; it is a living, breathing, growing plan.

> *"I don't believe in making plans.
> I love working in a natural flow."*

This statement may reveal a client who's evading responsibility. By saying and believing this, your clients don't make themselves responsible for achieving results. If they don't yet need to make a profit, then they don't have to make it happen. If there's no plan, no goal, then they can't fail. If you think this may be the case with your client, you must find out, otherwise you can't move on. Entrepreneurship does entail going with the flow and adapting to circumstances, both positive and negative, but that's not the whole story. You need a strategic plan to achieve desired results.

*"By the time the plan is finished,
it will have become obsolete."*

Entrepreneurs who say this are often thinking of a thick report called a "business plan" that they had to submit when they started their business or needed financing. A profit plan is nothing like that. First of all, a profit plan often fits on one or two pages. You won't spend weeks or months making the profit plan. It can be ready in half a day and it will provide immediate insight. Finally, it is a living document. If your plans change, the numbers change accordingly. A profitable plan is designed to evolve and will never become obsolete.

5.2 Making a profitable plan

Once you've overcome your clients' resistance to the notion of a profit plan, it's time to get to work! You'll want to reserve at least half a day for the first draft of the plan and give your client a homework assignment in advance.

Homework in advance

A homework assignment in advance is important for both you and the entrepreneur. You will receive the information you need to prepare for the meeting. And if you want to take big steps during the meeting, the entrepreneur must have thought about several things in the weeks prior to the meeting. By reflecting on the questions you ask, your clients will develop new insights and ideas. With the homework assignment done, you'll be prepared to be productive right from the start.

Typically, the homework assignment should consist of a questionnaire and a request to send you preliminary figures.

Questionnaire

You can partly tailor the questions you want to ask to the

entrepreneur you are working with. An entrepreneur who sells a physical product gets different questions than one in the service industry. You pose different questions to someone who has been successful in business for ten years than to a start-up. You try to standardize the basic questionnaire so that it takes you as little time as possible to deliver value to each client anew. The clearer you have defined your ideal client, the easier it is to draw up a standard questionnaire.

I'll give you several topics around which you can build your own questions:

1. *Mission and vision* – Ask your client to explain their mission (why do you do what you do?) and vision (where are you going?) in a few lines.

Your clients cannot ponder mission and vision often enough. They should remember the reason they're in business in the first place and the great goals they want to achieve. This is an essential start for making a profit plan.

2. *Unique offering* – Ask your clients why people do business with them, rather than the competition. Just like mission and vision, your clients should know their unique offering[2] and how to describe it. It forms the foundation of the plans you'll develop.

3. *Who is your ideal client?* – Ask your clients who their ideal client is. If this ideal client were to turn up on the doorstep right now, who would that be?

4. *What problems do you solve?* – Ask your clients to describe what problems they're solving with their service or product. Your clients are probably inclined to think in terms of actions and processes ("I'm a marketer, I'm a lawyer, I'm a web designer") rather than in terms of the problems they solve.

5. *Solution/product* – Ask your clients to name the concrete

product they sell. These products should logically be an answer to the problems described in point 4. If not, the client has just had a powerful feedback moment. You have just helped your clients take a step toward profit.

6. *Goal for the coming year* – What do your clients want to do in the coming year? What do they want to sell, produce or develop?

7. *Obstacles/challenges* on the way to your goal – What obstacles or challenges does your client already see?

Ask your client to send you the answers to the questions no later than three days before the meeting, and make sure those answers arrive. By setting a deadline, you're helping your client to take the required steps.

The meeting

Set aside half a day to a day to make the profit plan together. Don't shortchange this step. You will need that time. Also, try to make this meeting memorable.

Don't sit in a boring office, but invite your client to a beautiful outdoor location, with good coffee and a nice lunch. Give your clients a real VIP treatment. This will help you take them, yourself, and their plans seriously. Chances are that working in an inspiring environment will also have a positive impact on the results you will achieve. Finally, your client will begin to see you more and more as a profit advisor and not just as an accountant.

In the run-up to the meeting you can prepare several things:

- If you have an overview of your client's costs, put the overhead costs your client incurs in an Excel version of the profit plan.[3]
- This preparation helps you enormously with question 5 below.

- Bring enough post-its and markers with you. These are needed for question 2 below.
- Put a large flipchart on the wall showing the months of the year from left to right. You need these for question 3 below.

The final product of the meeting is a detailed profit plan on one A4 sheet. The plan does not have to be complete yet, but you will have a first draft. During or right after the meeting, you create a digital version of the profit plan so that you can share it with your client at the end of the meeting.

Take the lead during the meeting and ask your client the following questions – in the following order:

1. Why do you do what you do and what do you want to achieve with it?

You begin with your client's mission and vision. It is essential to start the day with this. A plan that does not start from the Why of the entrepreneur is an empty plan. A powerful Why provides energy and direction. It may be somewhat scary to ask these "vague" questions, but I haven't met an entrepreneur who doesn't know what to do with it. And the hundreds of profit plans that were made with my support all have a particularly solid foundation because we always start with the Why question. If the homework questions revealed illogical answers or raised further questions, this is the time to address your clients' unique offering, their ideal client and the problems they solve for their ideal client.

2. What are you going to sell in the next twelve months?

Ask clients to name all the products and services they want to sell. Ask them to write down each product or service on a separate post-it and stick the post-its on the table in front of them. Entrepreneurs generally really like to take this step. Everything they have worked through in their heads a hundred times is now shown on paper. That gives peace and insight.

3. When are you going to sell what?

Let the entrepreneur stick the post-its on the flipchart sheet you put on the wall during the preparation. This step also provides good insight. Entrepreneurs often come to the conclusion that they want much more than is reasonably possible in the available time. In this step it is also important to ask for the "quantity". How many new websites will your client develop in January? How many new clients register for coaching program X each month? Write down these products and the corresponding numbers in the digital version of the profit plan. As a side note: Tell your client what you are doing, otherwise you risk having him think that you are writing emails or are otherwise distracted.

4. What is the price of your services/products?

You ask the entrepreneur to set a price for each product. This can be a price per hour, per product or per program. If this price is not yet clear, let the entrepreneur quote a price based on gut feeling or current price.

Another homework assignment will be determining a clear price based on the cost price / time investment and the value that the product has for the end user. If it fits within the agreements you have with your client, you can also set the price together later.

Questions 3 and 4 are a challenge for both the entrepreneur and most profit advisors. This is because questions are raised that cannot be answered straightaway. Your clients don't yet know exactly what the right price is, or they may find it difficult to estimate how much they will sell of this or that product. Keep encouraging them to give their best answer. It is not a question of putting the truth on the table; the most important goal is to put on paper what's inside the entrepreneur's head. That gives you information to build on.

Write down the prices mentioned in the digital plan. This step is only completed when there is a first draft of the sales the client will make, specified by the underlying products and the months in which the product is sold. Do not yet share the results with your client at this stage, because they will just be distracting.

5. What costs do you need and want to incur to achieve your goals?

Now ask clients what costs they must and want to incur to realize this plan. I stress "want to", because costs often feel like something negative. But in order to achieve goals, investments almost always must be made. That may just as well be regarded as something positive.

During the preparation, you already put the overhead costs in the Excel version of the profit plan. In general, clients won't initially mention ongoing costs like the telephone bill and the rent. If they do, challenge them to look at costs that aren't there now but that are necessary for achieving goals. Should new staff be recruited? How many? And what will that cost? Do you need to invest in machines or software?

What investment – in the entrepreneur's estimate – will this require? Again, it is not relevant to dive too much into the details. Don't let clients get sidetracked by looking up exact software prices; stay focused on what's relevant. What is relevant is noting – on paper – that there will be a software investment, including an initial indication of the costs. The details will be entered later.

6. What net salary do you want to earn every month?

Whether your client is a sole proprietor or a corporation doesn't really matter for this question. You assume that everyone wants to earn a decent salary. After all, who's your client's best employee? Hint: it's him or her! The question is: how high should that salary be? Depending on fiscal rulings, which differ greatly per country and legal form, you should input the salary in the profit plan.

7. Which buttons should we press for the right result?

Now we have a first draft of the profitable plan. If you have succeeded in typing along with the entrepreneur, you can calculate the first global profit amount. It will give the entrepreneur valuable insight if you immediately make an initial global tax calculation on the basis of this profit. Now you can see at a glance whether your client's plans are feasible. Is the client making money?

If the result is not positive, meaning the company runs at a loss or not enough salary can be paid, then you need to fine-tune the plan. Chances are that you already knew that your client's costs were too high, but your client didn't want to hear that. Now it's obvious, thanks to the plan, that costs are too high in relation to the sales... and that makes an impact.

When your calculation shows your clients that their company isn't currently able to make a profit, there are a limited number of options: the sales must be increased (more products/services and/or a higher price per product or service) or the costs must be reduced. There are no other options. This can be a pretty uncomfortable moment for clients. But in my experience, this step is one of the most helpful in terms of spurring real change that leads to real profit.

At the end of the meeting, you give your clients the first draft of their profit plan. Email it on the spot. As an expert, you may feel inclined to take a look at it yourself before sending it, but if you are sure that the formulas are correct and you have processed everything your clients mentioned, then they should be the first to have it. If you immediately email it, they take ownership of it right from the beginning. It's their plan, not yours. Of course, you can provide support and assistance, especially if that fits within the process you have laid out, but that will come later! For now, encourage your clients to try to figure it out for themselves for a while.

5.3 Managing with the profit plan!

A profit plan is a living document. It's not finished after you've worked on it for half a day, and in fact, it's never really finished. To be "finished" is not the plan's objective. Understanding the consequences of choices and doing the right things are the important goals of the profit plan.

Feedback thanks to the plan

The weeks following the meeting can be quite uncomfortable for your clients. The entrepreneurial life continues, and all too often in real life the results that looked so good on paper are not achieved. Your clients may be disappointed and believe that making plans doesn't work. Don't let this discourage you. It is not so much that making a plan doesn't work; it is more that your clients are getting feedback in light of their plans. Only when they actively set the goal of finally making a balanced contribution to the family income will it hurt when they fail. Only when they set the goal of generating income passively will it hurt if that doesn't show.

Only when they have said out loud (and written down) that they will finally launch that new product and have been disappointed by results will it hurt. If entrepreneurs don't set any goals, they won't be disappointed by the results. At the same time, they will not achieve the desired results. It's really up to your clients which alternative they find most satisfying. My experience is that setting goals ultimately leads to more success than not setting them.

Your clients now have feedback, and they have decisions to make. They must take the feedback seriously and draw conclusions. Your most important role in this process is to establish and name the facts (what do the actual results tell you?) and ask the right questions about them. For more guidance on asking the right questions, see also chapters 9 and 10.

If you have a monthly meeting, that's the perfect moment to put their actual figures next to their plan. Where are the major differences? And above all, where do the desired results get achieved? As soon as you see that a product doesn't sell, certain costs are far too high or something else deviates significantly, you must identify the issue and ask questions about it. The purpose of asking these questions is not so much to get answers, but much more to make your clients think. They must act, not you.

Managing in response to the feedback

Encourage your clients to find the cause of their problems. What is the reason why the product doesn't sell or sells badly? What is the reason why the costs are much higher than anticipated? Now prompt your clients to come up with concrete solutions. What will they change now that the results are short of their goals? What will they do to ensure that a particular product sells? Or should they conclude that the product doesn't offer a solution to the client's problem? Can they modify the product? Or, if the costs are too high: how can they achieve the same results with lower costs? What happens if they delete a certain cost item?

It is not up to you to come up with the solutions; that is your clients' job. But asking questions makes them actively think about the solutions and focus on the results they want to achieve.

Sometimes plans just aren't realistic. Especially when clients keep on saying month after month, "It'll be all right," while nothing changes in the facts or figures, it is time to confront the client with the truth. At some point, entrepreneurs must face reality. They may be too optimistic, and this excessive optimism is damaging the health of their business. Sometimes entrepreneurs need to be encouraged to adjust sales plans downwards. When clients adjust their profit plan accordingly, they immediately see the effect of the changes on their profit.

Action step

Decide how you want to help your clients create a profitable plan. Add your own vision, knowledge, experience and systems to the information in this chapter and create your own unique product as part of your program.

In this chapter you were given the tools to help entrepreneurs translate goals, dreams and ideas into a feasible and profitable plan. In the next chapter you will discover how Profit First helps them with the daily management of cash flow.

---

1. In October 2019 I wrote and published the book *Winstgevende Plannen* (*Profitable Plans*). It became a number one bestseller in the Netherlands within a week-and-a-half. I surely hope *Profitable Plans* will also be available in English soon.
2. Read *The Pumpkin Plan* written by my good friend and business partner, Mike Michalowicz, if you want to learn more about creating a unique offering and finding your ideal client.
3. At www.theprofitadvisor.eu you can find a user friendly and built-for-you Excel template of the profitable plan under "products".

6 MANAGING WITH PROFIT FIRST

* * *

Eradicate entrepreneurial poverty! - Mike Michalowicz

* * *

I wasn't very happy when we were back on the street, and Peter looked downright worried. He understood by now that he didn't have the most modern accountant. I felt his spirits sag. In the short time he had worked with me, his image of himself and his company had rotated 180 degrees. He thought he was a successful entrepreneur because his business did 300K in sales and was growing. In his mind, he was building a strong business because he "invested" every cent he earned into it, but now he realized that he was creating a cash-eating monster. He also noticed that the person who was supposed to help him with his finances only got him deeper and deeper into the morass. It was clear that Peter wasn't feeling so upbeat anymore. Fortunately, I was still confident, because I knew exactly what was needed to get out of this mess and build a profitable business!

After the debacle at the accountant's, we walked into a sandwich store. After a sandwich and a good cappuccino, when Peter had recovered a bit from the shock, I asked the manager if I could borrow four cups and a pile of sugar cubes. He gave me a puzzled look, but I was charming enough that I got what I asked for. I put down the four cups in front of Peter and put the pile of sugar cubes on the table.

"I'd like to ask you a question. Imagine that those sugar cubes represent your sales of the past year and that the cups represent the four goals for your money: 1) profit, 2) owners pay, 3) taxes and 4) expenses. Can you distribute the sugar cubes over the cups?"

Peter started to laugh, but then looked at me worriedly. "Seriously?"

"Absolutely," I said.

Peter pushed the first, second, and third cups toward me empty. He stuffed as many sugar cubes as possible into the fourth cup and moved it in my direction, saying: "Expenses."

We both remained silent for a moment. I saw that the penny had finally dropped for Peter. He realized at that moment that his sales had four goals, and not just one. It was there and then that Peter saved his company. He decided that he was going to fill the other cups too.

* * *

Now that the accounting foundation is in place and your clients, thanks to their profit plan, know exactly whether plans are making them money and what they must do to make those plans come true, it comes down to the daily management of the finances. When we talk about managing based on the correct financial information, then you might say: "The accounts are in order thanks to step 1. We have a plan thanks to step 2, so we're done!" Not so fast. Although we have an important foundation, it is not yet enough for the entrepreneur to make the right financial choices and increase profitability. In this chapter I'll show you why that's the case, and how Profit First[1] delivers exactly the information the entrepreneur needs.

6.1 What problem does Profit First solve?

The bookkeeping is in order and the information is up-to-date and directly accessible to the entrepreneur. And yet clients still fail to make the right choices. There are at least five main problems: the first problem is that entrepreneurs don't look at their books. The second problem is that the information in the books is pure fiction. The third problem is that not all the important information is in the books. In my view, the fourth and fifth problems have the greatest impact. Fourth, an entrepreneur is a human being and therefore makes emotional, rather than rational decisions. And fifth, entrepreneurs with financial problems fall into the survival trap of sales, sales, sales, which alone isn't enough to solve their problems. Let me explain the five problems in more detail.

1. The entrepreneur doesn't look at the books

Of course, there are parts of the accounting that your clients do study. There's a good chance they'll be looking at their sales at least once a week, thanks to the updated accounts and profit plan. With a bit of luck, they'll also glance at expenses and profit. But they rarely look beyond that. For example, the books simply state what the sales tax debt is as of today, but the entrepreneur does nothing with this information. When the sales tax return has been filed, the amount to be paid may be frightening.

Why don't entrepreneurs look at their accounts? Because most of them find financial statements, especially the balance sheet, too complicated.

They don't understand what these statements say, and if they understand them, after your clear explanation, they don't know what to do with them. It is something they consider less interesting than other aspects of their business.

2. *The figures in the books are fictitious*

Even if your clients do pay attention to their accounts, they may still find it a challenge to translate them into something meaningful enough to prompt action. Revenue, for example, is purely fictitious. It's not real money. If – according to his profit and loss account – the entrepreneur currently has a $100K revenue, but his largest client has not yet paid the $20,000 bill, there is a huge gap between the accounting revenue, $100,000, and the money actually received, $80,000. If, according to the profit and loss account, the entrepreneur has a $50,000 profit, but there is not a single cent in the bank, what is that profit worth?

Entrepreneurs with debts could, in theory, see from the balance sheet how high those debts are at that moment. But the balance sheet does not reveal how much of that debt can reasonably be paid down in a month. Clients who hold major product launches, resulting in huge sales peaks, can in theory see from "pre-invoiced sales" that they still have to work for the money they've already received. But before he understands that and translates it into the practical consequences for today... well, that simply won't happen.

3. Relevant information is missing

Some information is also completely missing. The accounts don't show the size of the income or corporate tax debt already owed. The books don't tell your clients what they need to know to make the right financial decisions every day and to increase their company's profitability.

4. Entrepreneurs make emotional, rather than rational decisions.

The fourth problem with accounting is that it does not reflect people's natural behavior. For hundreds of years, financial experts have been saying: "Entrepreneur, look at your accounts and make better choices," but entrepreneurs don't do it. They are human beings and, therefore, make few rational choices. We think we do, but in reality, the vast majority of our decisions are emotional in nature.

Research shows that a decision is often made in a fraction of a second in the limbic brain, which is where our emotions reside. Then we will explain this decision with the rational part of our brain, which is located in the neocortex. It therefore seems as if a decision was made deliberately and rationally, but that is by no means the case. Think back to the last car you bought. Was it not the case that you first wanted a specific car (that particular Audi, Volkswagen, or BMW) and then you started collecting evidence to justify your choice? When it comes to business decisions, they are usually not made any differently. Entrepreneurs decide to invest in something and then look for the evidence to justify to themselves and their shareholders that the investment is the right choice at that moment. The fact that there is no financial room in the budget is irrelevant. At that moment, a budget is a merely fictitious and theoretical concept.

5. Entrepreneurs fall into the survival trap

"My sales grow, but I don't see it reflected in my profit." This is a problem that many growing entrepreneurs encounter. They constantly have money worries. They survive check to check, waiting anxiously until a client pays an invoice, so they can pay their suppliers themselves. They receive a minimal or even nonexistent owner's pay. They lie awake at night because they don't know how much tax they must pay or how to get through the quiet summer months.

As soon as business owners, for whatever reason, are no longer able to pay their suppliers, they do everything in their power to raise money. More revenue, more sales. Because with that extra revenue they can pay their bills... at least, that's what they think. But they rarely solve problems this way. They're not addressing the reason why they couldn't pay the bills. As soon as sales increase, the scale of the problem grows just as fast. I have a client who plunged himself deeper and deeper into debt by only focusing on sales. He thought, "If I win that next deal, I can pay the bills." But the next deal generated new expenses. Those bills came on top of the already huge pile. On top of that came the sales tax debt, which increased with the growth in sales. He didn't address the underlying issue, i.e. that he is running a cash burning organization. Last year, he had a problem of $250,000 on an annual basis. Unless he tackles the causes, he will create a problem of nearly $1 million this year.

The solution: adapt the system

The solution is not to provide more information in the form of financial reports. Entrepreneurs don't look at the reports, and if they do, they don't use the reports to guide their decisions. Profit guru, Mike Michalowicz has created a solution. He writes, "Let's stop telling entrepreneurs to adapt their behavior – let's adapt the system to the entrepreneur. Let's make sure the system allows the entrepreneur to manage his finances, so that he always pays himself first, always makes a profit, always has sufficient reserves for the tax authorities and pays his bills on time."

Mike Michalowicz is an American bestselling author and founder of several multimillion-dollar companies, who found himself on the verge of bankruptcy not long after earning his first million. He had learned how to make money, but he had never learned how to keep it. While zapping through various TV channels, he stumbled over a fitness expert explaining why diets don't work. He saw a resemblance with his own money issues and decided, "There must be a different way!" and developed, inspired by the diet industry, the Profit First method.[2]

Profit First is a simple and accessible method that helps entrepreneurs manage their cash flow based on their bank accounts. The method is based on the jar system our parents and grandparents used decades ago: each financial goal has its own jar. My grandmother used to have a jar for the groceries, one for the rent and one for the extras for the children. When she went to the shop, she only took the contents of the jar for the groceries with her. She never used money that was intended for another purpose. The Profit First method works exactly the same, the only difference being that the jars are bank accounts and the goals are business goals. Entrepreneurs who work with Profit First have at least five business accounts: one INCOME account where all the money comes in and four accounts for the most important business purposes: PROFIT, OWNERS COMP, TAX and OPEX.

It is a controversial method because it does something that has no accounting or tax significance whatsoever. Profit First says literally: "Open a separate bank account for every purpose of your money." For financial experts, this often feels nonsensical at first because from an accounting point of view you're not actually gaining anything. Worse, it only creates red tape and a lot of internal transfers. But the system works! And how! Profit First already works for almost one hundred thousand entrepreneurs worldwide. The method is explained in the book *Profit First*. Below is a summary of the system.

6.2 The new formula and the four core principles of Profit First

Profit First works thanks to a new formula and four principles.

New formula

The ancient formula for calculating profit, although mathematically correct, is a formula that does not work in practice. The formula says: Sales − Expenses = Profit. It invites entrepreneurs to sell as much as possible and then incur all the costs necessary to run their business. That is exactly what entrepreneurs do: sell, sell, sell. As soon as the client pays the invoice, the business owner pays as many outstanding invoices as possible. In this formula, profit is a leftover. If you're lucky, there's some money left at the end of the ride. Many entrepreneurs pay themselves little or no owner compensation, and they're certainly not making a profit. But if you have to live off the leftovers as an entrepreneur, you never achieve the financial freedom you dream of.

The old formula encourages entrepreneurs to sell more, but no matter how much income they generate, they always find a way to spend that money. In addition, this formula allows the entrepreneur to focus on sales and expenses, and not on profit. Because of the primacy effect, we want to grow what comes first (sales and expenses), and we don't pay attention to what comes last (profit).

Because the old formula doesn't help entrepreneurs make a

profit, Mike Michalowicz turns the formula around with Profit First. The new formula is: Sales − Profit = Expenses. Mathematically speaking nothing changes, but emotionally it does! Entrepreneurs still must sell; there is no business without sales. After that, however, their attention turns to making a profit. They literally first secure their profit. The expenses must be paid from what is left after that.

If the company is not sustainable that way, something is not right in the earning model or strategy, and we must work on that. The state of the bank accounts provides very clear and accurate feedback on the company's financial health.

The profit distribution

"Taking profit first" is not only a theoretical reversal of the formula; it is a real, recurring action. When distributing the revenue over the various accounts, your clients first secure their profit. The entrepreneurs who work with Profit First unanimously tell me that this is one of the highlights of their week. Often, they can't wait to distribute the money again. It is very motivating to transfer money to the profit account and see this amount grow.

Once every quarter, entrepreneurs receive a profit distribution from the company. They allocate 50% to their profit account, and the other 50% is reserved. The profit distribution is a reward that business owners receive for the risks they take, their innovative power and hard work. It is the intention that this money should be used for something special. The money may not be returned to the company; it must only be used to create memories, buy something beautiful, go out for dinner, and so on. Because the profit distribution only takes place once every quarter, it's not something the entrepreneurs expect. Thus, the money will not be part of their normal reward; it really is an extra bonus.

Four principles

In addition to reversing the formula, Profit First works thanks to four principles, all of which have their origins in the diet industry.

Principle 1: Use small plates

In 2012, a report by Koert van Ittersum and Brian Wansink showed that the size of plates in America has increased by 23% in a hundred years. Because people like to fill their plate completely (and then empty it), this leads to an intake of 50 extra calories per day. This leads to a weight increase of approximately five pounds each year. The diet industry advises to eat from smaller plates if you want to lose weight. You then eat smaller portions, consume fewer calories and lose weight.

This is based on Parkinson's law, which says: "work expands so as to fill the time available for its completion." It applies in the same way to food, time, and money. You probably know that if your client gives you a week to complete a project, it takes a week to complete. At exactly 5 p.m. on Friday afternoon you finish the last line and press the send button. But if you are given just one day, it only takes one day... and often with the same result. You work more efficiently, and your efforts are more focused.

The more you have of something, the more you will use of it. That goes for everything: food, time, and certainly money. Have you ever had a pay raise? Maybe $100? Think back to this pay raise. At the end of the month in which you received this pay increase, did you have that $100 left? Probably not! Chances are that the money had all been spent: we use the available space.

In business terms, too, entrepreneurs use the available space.

They may think they're making sensible financial choices, but Parkinson's law also applies to their business. As more comes in, more goes out. It's that simple. *Profit First* recognizes Parkinson's law and says: "Let's adapt the system so that Parkinson's law works for, rather than against, entrepreneurs. Let's apply the 'small plates' principle to our clients' businesses."

As mentioned above, entrepreneurs working according to the Profit First rules do not work with one, but with at least five bank accounts: one bank account for each purpose: Income, Profit, Owner's comp, Tax, and Opex. Because your clients no longer have one bank account, a large plate, that their company can completely empty, they make much better choices. They first reserve their profit in a separate bank account. They do the same for their owner's compensation and the money they need to pay the tax authorities. Then they have a significantly smaller plate available to pay the expenses. Your clients make better choices because they must. They are more creative and don't spend money that isn't there.

Principle 2: Serve sequentially

The second principle also originates from the diet industry. If you want to lose weight, the advice is to eat vegetables first, so that you fill your stomach with healthy food, high in fiber and vitamins. Only then do you eat your potatoes with gravy, so you eat less of them. In Profit First, entrepreneurs always reserve profit first. They then reserve the salary for their best employee (themselves!). Then they set aside money for the tax authorities and finally, they put money in the Expense Account, from which they pay the suppliers. Only after all the money has been distributed over the various accounts, will your clients address expenses. This way, entrepreneurs take good care of themselves, don't have to worry about the taxes, and get firm feedback from the bank account if their company is overspending.

Principle 3: Remove temptation

If you don't want to eat candy, you must make sure you don't have any at home. Remove the temptation. It's that simple. The same goes for money. As soon as your clients begin applying the principles of Profit First, they start reserving money for specific purposes and, of course, that money is not supposed to be used for other purposes. Yet the temptation is often great. The tax plate, for example, sometimes quickly fills up with tens of thousands of dollars. For an entrepreneur, it may be very tempting to borrow from that plate. The tax may only have to be paid in a year's time, and that money could well be used for another purpose.

But in the end, borrowing money that is not his, but that of the tax authorities, will cause a lot of stress. One day he will have to pay the tax bill and the money will have to be there!

The third principle of Profit First urges business owners to remove the temptation by transferring the amount in question to a savings account with another bank. It is literally out of sight and out of mind! Although entrepreneurs initially sometimes hesitate and say: "Is that really necessary? I won't touch it," this proves to work really well in practice. Strangely enough, we seem to forget that we have deposited that money in another account, with the result that we aren't actually tempted to borrow it. Besides a "no temptation account" for the taxes, the advice is to also open a "no temptation account" for the profit. You reserve the portion of the profit that the entrepreneur does not distribute to himself. This reserve serves as a buffer for profitable investments or as a financial freedom fund.

Principle 4: Enforce a Rhythm

The fourth principle is rhythm. When you wait with eating until you're hungry, it is often too late because you then start eating unhealthy things. When it comes to accounting, the lack of rhythm is often disastrous. Entrepreneurs often have such aversion to their bookkeeping that they postpone working on it for as long as possible. The result is that the bookkeeping, when they finally do get around to it, causes them much stress and late nights.

The challenge is to teach your clients an accounting rhythm of one minute per day plus 30 minutes per week. This way, accounting becomes a habit and your client doesn't have to think about it. This way, accounting will ultimately cost less time and money, and will certainly cause less stress. Moreover, it will provide the desired insight!

Part of the daily rhythm is checking the balance on the various accounts. "Keeping a finger on the pulse" gives us a good idea of our company's financial health. We get a grip on how the money flows through the company during the month. During the weekly 30-minute accounting moment, we allocate receipts between the four accounts and pay the invoices out of the Opex account.

6.3 Implementing Profit First

Entrepreneurs often quickly recognize the usefulness and importance of Profit First. When I tell them about the method, I often hear them say, "Why didn't I think of that myself?" This method uses natural behavioral tendencies, so your clients will quickly get used to it. It is essentially also a very simple method, which doesn't necessarily mean that it is easy to implement. Implementing Profit First requires customization. Each entrepreneur's individual situation must be carefully considered: what is the company structure, how financially healthy or unhealthy is the company at the moment, what are the goals, how are the accounting processes structured? And so on.

Opening accounts

The first step in the implementation of Profit First is the opening of the five business bank accounts: Income, Profit, Owner's comp, Tax and Opex at your daily bank, and "no temptation" Tax Hold and Profit Hold Accounts at your second bank, Bank 2.

- *Income Account* – This is the account your revenue goes to. From this account, the money received is periodically distributed among the other accounts.
- *Profit Account* – When distributing the income to the other accounts, the profit is always reserved first.
- *Owner's Comp Account* – From this account the entrepreneur receives a monthly salary.
- *Tax Account* – This account is used to reserve both sales tax and income or corporate tax. Once every quarter a part of this reservation is transferred to the corresponding "no temptation" account at Bank 2.
- *Opex Account* – After the money has been distributed over the various accounts, the entrepreneur pays suppliers from this Operating Expenses Account.

Points of attention when opening multiple bank accounts

Not all banks encourage the opening of at least five bank accounts, and if they do offer the possibility, it is sometimes expensive.

On https://profitfirstprofessionals.com/resources/ you can read further advice on finding a bank that supports Profit First. It is also important that there is an automatic link with the entrepreneur's accounting software. It costs too much time and money if files have to be imported from all these accounts.

The Profit Assessment

The amounts transferred from the Income Account to the various other accounts are based on fixed percentages. These percentages differ per entrepreneur and per industry; they depend, for example, on the financial health and size of the company. In a Profit Assessment Target Allocation, percentages are calculated on an individual basis.

6.4 Profit First in practice

Once the percentages have been determined, the accounts opened, and – if applicable – clients and suppliers have been informed about changed account numbers, entrepreneurs can get started. They now manage money according to a fixed rhythm with daily, fortnightly, monthly and quarterly actions. They distribute income, pay the bills, receive profit distributions, etc. As a profit advisor, you should preferably check every quarter to ensure a sufficient amount has been reserved for tax on the "no temptation" Tax Account at Bank 2. If this is not the case, the tax percentage must be adjusted. I also recommend you take a close look at the other percentages every quarter and adjust them if necessary or possible.

Feedback from the bank

After entrepreneurs have been working with Profit First for a while, there arrives the moment Mike Michalowicz calls the "come to Jesus moment", the moment of truth. Newcomers to Profit First discover that their Operating Expenses Account is constantly empty, while bills still have to be paid. Or they notice they're always tempted to "borrow" money from other accounts; they may even do so. They may also find that the amount in the Owner's Pay Account is not enough to support their lifestyle. Entrepreneurs conclude that the system is not working, while the harsh reality is that they are confronted with their company's real financial situation. If the Opex Account is always empty while the bills have not yet been paid, then there is simply an unhealthy cost structure. If entrepreneurs incur more costs than the business can bear, either costs must be reduced or sales increased. There are no other options. Of course, clients can "borrow" from the tax account, but that money isn't really theirs. They will have to pay it back sooner or later. They can also reduce their salary or profit percentage, but that hurts.

The beauty of Profit First is that your clients experience this come to Jesus moment first hand. You may have told them on many occasions that their costs are too high, but they might have denied it. Perhaps they even thought you were being too conservative. But now that the bank account tells them that the money has run out, they see the truth.

The finer points of the system

In this chapter, I described the basis of the Profit First method. You can immediately apply the principles for the benefit of your clients. For example, advise them to reserve the sales tax and tax on profit owed in a separate account on a regular basis. Do you want to apply the method in full? Then you need a deeper understanding of the process. Please refer to www.profitfirstprofessionals.com for more information. A Profit First Professional membership will provide you with intense training and you will receive a certificate and a license to market yourself as a Profit First Professional.

The training answers all questions you may have after reading this chapter, and dozens more, including:

- How do you determine the company's current financial health?
- How do you do a Profit Assessment?

- What are ideal allocation percentages?
- What do you do with the money in your account when the entrepreneur starts Profit First?
- How do you deal with retirement reservations?
- How does investing work in combination with Profit First?
- How do you ensure that you reserve the correct amount for the tax payment?
- Can you divide the accounts over several banks?
- What do you do with an entrepreneur who purchases a lot?
- How do you deal with the profit distribution in an Inc.?
- What do you do with an entrepreneur with debts?
- Is Profit First different for starters than for experienced entrepreneurs?
- What other accounts can you use, in addition to the standard accounts, to help the entrepreneur manage his finances even better?
- How do you help the entrepreneur move from the current situation to the desired situation?

Action step

Would you like to know more about Profit First? Download the most important chapters of the book for free at https://profitfirstbook.com. Want more information about becoming a Profit First Professional? Please contact us at www.profitfirstprofessionals.com.

In this chapter, I told you about Profit First, a method that many entrepreneurs claim has saved their business. With accounting as a solid foundation and the profit plan as a guiding instrument, Profit First is for many entrepreneurs the third step on the road to a healthy and profitable company.

As soon as your services truly create additional value for your client, it is important that you get paid adequately for this added value. This is the subject of the next chapter.

---

1. *Profit First* is a book and a method by Mike Michalowicz. Read the book *Profit First* or go to ProfitFirstProfessionals.com to inquire about becoming a certified Profit First Professional yourself. Certification is available globally.
2. Mike Michalowicz described the method in detail in his book Profit First. I contributed to the Dutch version of the book and with his permission I will give you a summary of the system in this chapter. Would you like to work with Profit First with your clients? Then please visit: www.profitfirstprofessionals.com.

7 SELLING HIGH-PRICED ADVISORY SERVICES

* * *

The questions you ask are more important than the things you could ever say – Tom Freese

* * *

I hung up and for a while just stared into space, smiling. I'd just talked to Peter's accountant Greg, who had also become my client. He called to thank me.

"Your book *The Profit Advisor*, together with your support, saved my life," were his first words.

The nine months that had passed since that first meeting with Peter at Greg's office had been, in his own words, "tough". He was angry with me at first, but soon he realized that it wasn't me who had to change; he himself had to take action. He read *The Profit Advisor* and contacted me. He really went for it and had worked very hard the last few months. He asked dozens of clients about their real problems, examined his own processes, developed new services and defined his ideal client.

And just before he phoned me, he had, for the first time in his career as an accountant, brought in his first ideal client, Anne. This made his heart beat faster and – as the icing on the cake – this new client would pay him for the value he was going to provide. The rate Greg had asked was not only higher than ever before, it was also a much better reflection of the value he was going to offer Anne. This meant that he already knew that she would be on top of mind and would receive a lot of his attention and energy. Greg was already looking forward to the great results that Anne would achieve with his support.

The conversation with her was very different from what he was used to. During the conversation he had butterflies in his stomach because he felt with every fiber of his being that he could help this client increase her profits by at least 15%. He had wanted to shout at her, "BE MY CLIENT", but he didn't have to.

At the end of the 45-minute conversation, after Greg had made an investment proposal, she said without any reservations: "That sounds like a great proposal. Let's do it." Greg was on cloud nine. And he just wanted to let me know that.

* * *

One of my clients, Corinne, a big city accountant, participated in my program to become a Profit Advisor for about six months and she had made great progress. During that time, she became a certified Profit First Professional, identified her ideal client, and developed a unique program. Then Corinne sent me this email:

Hi Femke,
My problem is marketing and selling my program.
I still have a lot to learn in this area. Even though I am now a profit consultant, as a former accountant, I am not used to selling myself online.
Regards, Corinne

Corinne's previous clients used to come through recommendations by others or via Google. They were looking for an accountant, and Corinne was an accountant. She had a modern website and asked prices in line with the market. When Corinne and the prospective client hit it off in the introductory meeting, Corinne had a new client.

Now that she was a profit advisor, things had changed. She knew who her ideal client was, and more importantly, she had what was needed to solve her client's real problems. Doing the books was the foundation, and that worked without requiring too much time, money and energy. Her real added value was in helping her clients make a profit, work more efficiently, pay off debts, and more. But her potential clients didn't know that. They didn't yet realize that they needed a profit advisor. They thought they needed an accountant.

Corinne faced a double challenge: she had to sell her new program and services, and she wanted to be paid better than before. Her new services were of great value to her clients, and Corinne wanted to get paid for the value she added. She gained in-depth knowledge of her clients and therefore knew more, much more, than her colleagues about the challenges they were facing. She invested time and money in her own growth, provided tailor-made solutions, thought of her clients when she was on her way to the gym and often helped clients earn thousands of dollars. She wouldn't dream of doing that for just

$80 per hour. Her challenge was how to get these clients to find her, buy her program and pay a good price for it.

In this chapter you will learn how to attract the right prospective clients with content marketing, and why you should not have an introductory interview with them but a consultative call. Finally, you will learn step by step how to conduct such a conversation.

7.1 How do you get premium fees?

If you sell waffles on the market, apart from tasty waffles, you don't need much more than a sign that says, "Waffles", and you are in business. If you want someone to pay you $1,000 per month instead of $80 per hour, you need more than a website that states that you are an accountant.

American marketing consultant John Jantsch defines marketing as: "Getting someone who has a need, to know, like and trust you." First of all, your potential clients need to know you. They need to know that you are there and that you are offering what they need. Then they need to like you and want to get to know you better. Finally, they need to trust you. They must feel that you understand and can help them. Every potential client must go through these three phases, known as Know-Like-Trust, before becoming your client.

The sales funnel

If you always and consistently go through these phases, you will always get clients. I learned that from Sabia, a top saleswoman I met when I had just started my own business. Sabia and I had a lunch appointment, and on the back of a coaster she drew the so-called sales funnel (see Figure 4). If you make sure that you continuously set out actions at every level of the funnel, you'll always get clients at the bottom end of the funnel. There is no other way. That is the law of selling, according to Sabia.

Figure 4: The sales funnel

The sales funnel includes the following parts:

- *Audience* – In the space above the funnel you give the audience the opportunity to get to know you. People hear about you through social media channels, they see your ads, or they hear you speak at a network meeting. This is the Know phase.
- *Leads* – If these people get the idea that you may be able to help them solve their problem, they move from the Know phase to the Like phase. They don't immediately become clients, but they would like to get to know you better. They subscribe to your newsletter, send you an email or follow your free online training.
- *Prospects* – The funnel gets narrower and narrower toward the bottom. That makes sense – not everyone who hears about you will eventually become your client. The better you have defined your ideal clients, the sooner they recognize that what you offer is relevant to them personally and the easier and faster they continue to the next phase in the funnel: the Trust

phase. This is the phase in which people trust you and show you they're open to buying from you. They want to talk to you, request a quote or buy an accessible, low priced product from you, such as a cheap online training or an introductory workshop.
- *Clients* – You offer your program to the people who talk to you. If you have succeeded in talking to the right people and piqued their interest, and you always pay enough attention to each level in the funnel, then it is inevitable that clients will emerge from the bottom end of the funnel. That is the law of selling.

Selling from the heart

Many entrepreneurs find marketing and sales difficult and challenging. They think marketing means constantly harassing people with your product, while they are not interested at all. You have to brag and make yourself bigger than you are. Selling does not have a good reputation either. Everyone has experienced a telemarketer trying to get you a new newspaper subscription. Selling is often synonymous with imposing something on someone.

As long as you see marketing and sales in this way, it will be difficult for you to sell your services. And that is not only a problem for you, but for your ideal clients too. You've gone to the trouble of refining what you offer – real solutions for real problems. If you don't sell your services, you deny your ideal clients an important opportunity. If, on the other hand, you sell from the heart – that is, you enter into a dialogue with the client to find out what his real problem is and whether you can help him solve it – selling becomes a process that benefits all parties. It helps you because you are in business and get to make your mission known to the wider world; and it helps your clients because they get a clear view of their problems and desires and because you give them the opportunity to work toward a solution.

Below, I will discuss content marketing, a marketing method that focuses on value sharing. Finally, I will explore the sales talk and how you can conduct it from your heart.

7.2 Content marketing

Marketing is making your company, service or product visible to the right target group, so your ideal client will get to know you, like you, and trust you – and eventually buy your product. You can market your company, service, or product by placing advertisements, having a presence on social media, blogging, and so on, but you're likely to encounter several major problems if you do this without a clear plan. Your risk of being ignored is considerable, and if you do a little bit of everything, you won't achieve anything.

Avoid being ignored

We live in an information society where we are literally flooded with information. To avoid being overwhelmed by so much information, we filter out most of it. We ignore information that does not stand out or that does not seem relevant.

To be seen by your potential client, you must avoid being ignored. If you see marketing as the continuous promotion of your services and products, the audience will ignore you. Most consumers simply aren't interested in advertisements. Seeing marketing as constantly telling people what they can buy from you thus has little effect. What does work very well, however, is sharing relevant information, information that really benefits your ideal client. This is called content marketing. You share your knowledge and show that you are an expert. Potential clients learn from you, they trust you and are curious to learn more from you. Their next logical step is to buy something from you. Content marketing is versatile, as it's not strongly tied to a particular marketing medium, and it works especially well if you succeed in reaching potential clients over and over again.

Which subjects lend themselves to content marketing?

"What should I talk about?" is a concern often expressed by bookkeepers and accountants who want to do more with content marketing. Two issues often underlie this concern. First, accountants believe that everything has already been said in their profession. That may be so. You can find lots of information about everything on the Internet. But there is only one person who presents information in your way, based on your why. Secondly, financial experts are afraid that after three blogs they will run out of material. This particular fear often proves to be ungrounded. If you take a little time you can easily write down 20 questions that you get asked regularly by email or during network meetings. And there you have your first 20 articles, vlogs, or tips. If you actively search for topics, then the sky is your limit.

Let people see the real you

People buy from people. Potential clients are more likely to feel a connection with you if they feel they really have meaningful contact with you and get to know you. That means you must show the real you. Don't try to copy someone who seems to be successful in your industry. That's not authentic, and potential clients will sense that. Don't try to be too businesslike or too general, either. If your article could have been written by anyone, it's a lot less attractive than when your personality, your

Why can be read in every line of your article. Show yourself, dare to be vulnerable and speak and write from your Why!

Select consciously

Content marketing can be done on all possible media. You can be active on Facebook or Instagram. You can blog, vlog, make podcasts, or write a newsletter. You can sponsor the local sports club, buy radio time, advertise in trade journals, and much more. But if you do a little bit of everything, you will probably get zero effect. It is not enough for potential clients to hear from you once. They need to hear from you regularly before they know you, like you and believe you're the right person to work with.

It is essential that you ask yourself on which media you want to present yourself to your potential clients. Do some research into where you can find your ideal client, and also think about which medium suits you best and where you already have experience. It is often smartest to simply start at a place where you are already visible and branch out to new channels from there.

The money is in the list

Just placing an advertisement is like firing buckshot. The chance that it will yield something is minimal. You don't know if your ideal clients will see the ad, and if they do see it, whether the ad will spur them into action. Sending an email to someone who has indicated that they are your ideal client is perfect! This is where an important proverb of online business comes in: The money is in the list. It means that it pays to draw up a list of potential clients that you can email. You can then provide them with valuable information on a regular basis. You will cultivate the relationship. People will start to see you as an expert, and you will create trust. But you don't just give away information, you also offer your services and products. Now we are talking about targeted marketing, because you only mail your ideal clients and they have indicated themselves that they are interested in what you have to say. It doesn't get any better than that.

You can create an email list in different ways. You can literally ask people you know if you can put them on your list. But at the end of the day you want your list to be drawn up as efficiently as possible. What works very well is offering something valuable in exchange for an email address. Be careful, because if you are going to give away conversations, there is a limit to the amount of new registrations you can handle. Think of a free e-book, a free online training, a checklist or anything else that is scalable and suitable for digital distribution. For example, you can offer your freebie through social media channels, network meetings, and partners.

Technical and legal aspects of creating a list

The technical side of creating a list is not very difficult, but it does require some technical knowledge and the use of modern technologies. Basically, you need an autoresponder (a system that automatically sends emails), and an opt-in on your website that you link to that autoresponder. It is also important to ensure that you comply with the legal requirements regarding the privacy of personal data. When doing business with companies in the European Union, make sure you comply with the General Data Protection Regulation (GDRP), which imposes strict requirements on the collection and use of email addresses and other personal data.

Ways to share knowledge

Besides structurally creating an email list, there are many more ways to share knowledge and work on your expert status. Think of, for example:

- writing blogs
- vlogging
- Facebook live
- recording podcasts
- appearing as a guest in other people's podcasts
- writing articles for trade journals
- sharing tips
- writing books
- writing e-books
- creating online training courses
- creating checklists
- giving webinars
- giving talks at network meetings

Much of the content you create can be used in various ways. When you record a podcast, you can both invite new listeners to subscribe to your newsletter and send newsletter readers a link to that podcast. The same goes for your e-book, vlogs, Facebook live events and so on. You create the content once and then use it over and over again.

Create a marketing plan

If actively marketing your knowledge and services is quite new to you, the amount of possibilities can be overwhelming. Make a plan and start small. Start with something you already do or can do, or perhaps something you've been wanting to explore.

Make sure you master one thing before you tackle the next. Ask yourself the following five questions:

1. Where is my ideal client?

2. Which way of marketing appeals to me? Do I like to write? Do I like to record videos? Or do I like to draw visuals?

3. Which medium that I am already using would I like to develop further?

4. What is the first step I will take this week?

5. What do I want to achieve in the field of marketing within a quarter?

Don't make it too big. It is better to do one thing well than three things by halves. As a Russian proverb says: "If you chase two rabbits, you will not catch either one."

7.3 Consultative selling

Ultimately, you want your visibility to lead to new clients. You want to sell your high-priced services. You want to talk to potential clients, so that you can make them an offer, if appropriate. Make sure you have weekly conversations with potential clients. In this section, I will consider two questions, i.e. how to get to talk to potential clients and how to conduct those conversations.

How do you get in touch with potential clients?

Invite them. The law of selling dictates that the sales funnel will generate clients. There is no other way. So, invite potential clients to talk to you. You can accomplish this in several ways:

Call potential clients

If you sit down for ten minutes, you will probably produce a list of ten to twenty contacts you would like to have as a client. Create that list and call the names on it. You shouldn't aim to immediately convert clients with these conversations. Because potential clients aren't prepared for this conversation, they may feel overwhelmed rather than ready to become your client. It's often smarter to talk for a few minutes to find out how they're doing and if they're still struggling with the problem you think they have. If you discover they can benefit from your expertise, make a new appointment – either for a call or a face to face meeting. Explain that the purpose of that conversation is to discuss their problem in more detail and to see if you can help them solve it. Your potential clients will then know exactly where they stand. Both you and your prospect will be prepared and on the same page.

Email potential clients

Instead of calling your potential clients, you can also email them. That takes less time, but an email is easier to ignore than a phone call, so the effect will be smaller. If you have an email list, you can also send a general email, in which you discuss the problems you expect your ideal client is facing. You will also indicate in it that you would like to talk to them. For example, you can send an email describing a common problem shared by your clients, so that one individual may recognize his or her own situation in it. A substantive article, a testimonial or five concrete tips to solve the identified problem, are all good ways to get clients interested in talking to you. Then you indicate that you have a method to tackle this problem. Finally, you invite the potential client for a face-to-face meeting. This can be done, for example, as follows: "Do you recognize yourself in this problem and are you curious about how I can help you with it? I would like to have a no-obligation talk with you. Reply to this email and I will contact you as soon as possible to schedule an appointment."

Networking meetings

Have you run into your ideal clients at a networking meeting? Then invite them to continue the conversation at a later time and pull out your diary straightaway. You should be aware that many people will really appreciate your willingness to talk to them. You offer a lot of value, if only by helping people clarify their problems.

Give webinars

A webinar is a great way to provide a lot of value to a large group of potential clients at the same time. You prepare a valuable webinar where you share concrete tips about a specific problem, and you invite potential clients via social media or your email list to attend this webinar for free. Since you can't solve all the problems in one hour, you can invite people at the end of the webinar to make an appointment with you to continue the conversation. It is best if people can schedule the appointment themselves in your calendar via an online meeting tool. You can share its URL during the webinar.

Online

You can also set up appointments online. This means that you will use online channels such as Facebook and LinkedIn to get potential clients interested in a conversation with you, and you will then let them schedule a meeting themselves via an online meeting tool. If the content you post is good and you manage to attract the right audience, you can easily arrange weekly conversations with potential clients this way.

How to make a consultative call?

Inviting potential clients to a conversation is one thing. Conducting the conversation in such a way that the right people become clients and are willing to invest in a solution is another thing. The formal start of the relationship is traditionally done through an introductory meeting. "We must hit it off," say both financial experts and their potential clients about the terms of cooperation. During the interview, the prospects talk about their wishes and you, the financial expert, talk about what you can offer. But this is not enough if you want to sell higher-priced consultancy services. In this case, prospects must have a clear-cut understanding of their problem, what the costs of the problem are, and that you are the right party to help solve it. They must understand that the investment you ask for is lower than the price of not solving the problem. You understand, of course, that this requires more than just an introductory meeting.

You must avoid falling into the pitfall of telling your prospective clients during the introductory meeting what you can do for them. If you start talking from your universe: "This is the package we work with, we provide the following reports...," then you just have to hope that what you offer is in line with the prospects' wishes. Your prospects are likely to feel like they're being offered a standard package. Even if that is the case, because you prefer to offer standardized packages, your clients need to feel like they're being handled as individuals, that their particular problems can be solved by your particular expertise. You will be much more effective if you first let prospective clients tell you what their problems and wishes are, rather than giving them the feeling that they have to comply with your standards.

So, begin by asking questions. Let your client do the talking while you ask more questions. Don't cut your prospects off after their first answer and start explaining how you plan to solve all their problems. That's not really listening; that's listening for the purpose of being able to talk. Active listening means that you want to understand exactly what your prospective client wants and needs. So continue asking, "What else?" Listen not only to discern your prospects' needs but also to assess whether a prospect is your ideal client with problems you're equipped to solve. Finally, you should know that people like to talk. If you let your prospects talk, they'll trust you and be more likely to choose you as their trusted advisor.

The form of conversation I am discussing here is called the "consultative call". A consultative call is not an intake or sales call. Although the call can produce a new client, it is not your goal to sell here. The first objective of a consultative call is to get a complete picture of the prospect's situation, so that you can give professional advice that's tailored to your prospects' needs. An offer to work with you can be the outcome of such a conversation, but just as often it will have a different outcome. When you start making consultative calls, it is not your intention to attract as many clients as possible, but to give your client the best advice based on your mission. As soon as you speak to your ideal clients, people whose business you can help grow, then – and only then – will you do everything you can to recruit those people as clients. If they don't become your client, then it is a loss not only for you but for them too.

When selecting the first Profit First Professionals for my program, I spoke to 34 prospects following a thorough pre-screening. I advised five of them to take another step. These were mostly starters, whom I advised to set up their company first. I made an offer to the other 29. Four of them decided for themselves that this was not the right step for them, and 25 people started the training. Had selling been my only goal, I would probably have started with 27 or even 28 or 29 clients. But not all of them would have been my ideal clients, so I would not have been able to deliver the value that I do now.

The purpose of a consultative call is to create trust and determine whether there is a match and if you want to make an offer. Such a conversation lasts on average one hour and can be conducted by telephone, via an online meeting tool or face to face.

The right mindset

The most important ingredient for a successful conversation is the right mindset. A conversation gets a rather heavy load when it absolutely must produce a new client. You will be putting a lot of pressure on yourself, and the client will probably feel that pressure too. Worse still, you will not be leaving the possibility open that you may not want the person in question as a client after all.

A better mindset is that you will investigate together what the real problems are and whether you're the right person to solve them. If that is the case, you make an appropriate offer. And if you are not the right person to help at that moment? Then you don't make an offer and finish the conversation.

Laura Babeliowsky, a Dutch business coach, taught me the term "passionately detached". And I find it a wonderful description of the right mindset. I choose to approach conversations with my prospects with passionate detachment. That means that I have the sincere intention to get to the heart of the matter. I really want to know what they are up against, what their challenges, struggles, and desires are. At the same time, I am completely detached from the outcome of the conversation. I am not engaged in "bringing in" a client. I make an offer to work with me if I believe I can really help. And it is up to them to accept or decline my offer. It is your responsibility to make the offer to the prospect. It is the other party's responsibility to accept or decline that offer.

The parts of the consultative call

In the consultative call you will explore your prospects' current situation, main problems and goals. You decide, preferably during the conversation, whether you want to make an offer and if so, which one. In the ideal situation, it will be clear at the end of the conversation whether or not you are going to work together.

Your prospects also get a clear view of their problems and goals, which is of value in itself. Often, they have a general feeling of dissatisfaction or stress, without knowing exactly what the real problem is and what steps to take. During the conversation with you, they'll get a clear view of their situation. This makes the consultative call a valuable conversation for your prospect.

I am going to share different parts of the consultative call. Don't stick too rigidly to the order of the parts of the consultative call. The parts described here are intended as a guide to help you discuss what's important. Sometimes at the start of the conversation it turns out that prospects first want to know more about you before they describe their own situation. If you stick to a predetermined order at that moment, you may find prospects unwilling to open up and share. Turn the order around and answer their questions first.

Preparing for the conversation

Preparation is half the battle. By immersing yourself in your prospects' situation beforehand, you create a double advantage for yourself: you already know them a little, which makes the conversation easier and more focused, and the other party feels seen and heard, which is extremely important if they are to trust you. Before the interview, take the time to study the information you have about your prospect. Did they e-mail you useful information beforehand? Did they complete a questionnaire? Take a look at their website and LinkedIn profile.

1. Lay out the agenda

You are in charge. Make sure you take charge and stay in charge. Explain the purpose of the conversation and how much time you have set aside for it. Explain that you have questions so that you can get to know them and their challenges, and that you are also happy to answer any questions they might have. Also make it clear that at the end of the conversation, if appropriate, you would like to explain how your expertise can help.

I once failed to manage expectations at the beginning of the meeting. Before I knew it, my conversation partner had taken over entirely and asked me to help her with her accounting software. Although I like to give concrete tips and advice in a consultative call, this was not my intention for that particular call. In the end, this conversation failed to produce the desired effect for either party. She may have received free answers to several concrete questions, but I could have helped her much better if she had become a client. This experience strengthened me in my decision to always clearly manage the expectations in advance.

2. Get to know the prospect

Ask questions, ask more questions, and then ask a few more questions. Asking questions is crucial at this stage. By asking the right questions, you can achieve two essential things:

- The other party feels seen and heard, and you establish trust.
- You get to know the prospects sufficiently well so that you can decide whether you can or can't make them the right offer.

How to become an expert in asking questions is taught in chapters 9 and 10. In this section I will show you several concrete questions that will help you get to know the prospect.

Question 1: What problem do you solve for whom and how?

People often use the following opening sentence: "Tell me something about yourself and your company." That's a broad and unfocused assignment. The answer can go any direction and it can take a long time before you know what the client actually does. The question you ask determines the answer you get. If you ask better questions, you will get better answers.

When you ask "What problem do you solve for whom, and how do you solve it?" you get quick and good insight into what kind of company your clients have, who their ideal client is, and what value they deliver to clients. Don't be satisfied with the answer too quickly. Continue asking questions. If you really want to help your clients build a financially healthy and profitable business, you need to know exactly how they make their money.

Don't underestimate the value you provide to your client with these questions. You're helping prospect refine their goals and sharpen their focus, which gives you quite a few bonus points compared to the old-school accountant who only asks which accounting system they use and whether they keep track of their hours.

Question 2: Tell me a little more about your company. Do you have any staff? How big is your company? How long has it been operating?

Now you begin collecting more general information about the company, so that you will get fuller understanding of current operations.

Question 3: Can you tell me something about the company finances?

In order to make a good assessment of the problem and to be able to make a suitable offer, it is important to have a clear picture of the financial situation of the client's company. Among other things, information about sales, profit, debts and margins is very relevant. But information about the private situation, such as pension accrual, regularity and amount of the salary and whether there are any money worries is also important.

Question 4: What is your biggest challenge at the moment?

This is a broad question and it usually brings the most important issues to the fore. These problems can lie in many areas: debt problems, declining margins, too low an income, legal problems, high staff costs, and so forth. Dare to keep asking. The answers to this question often highlight what added value you can provide. So write down the biggest problems! Is a prospect the breadwinner with unreliable income? There lies your added value. Is the margin falling? Are there debts? Has nothing been arranged yet for retirement? Do they want to hire staff? This information helps you ask a much better price for your services at the end of the consultative call.

Question 5: Why does ... <answer to question 4> require your attention?

With this question you challenge prospects to indicate how bad their problems actually are and how heavily those problems weigh on their minds. If you are going to make them an offer later, you want them to understand how badly they need your help. Confronting their problems helps prospects identify this need, so it's important that they formulate their own answers to this question. It is not up to you to describe their problems; it's up to them. If your prospects say they have a $200,000 tax debt, it is considerably more powerful if they tell you it keeps them awake at night than it is for you to remark on their large tax obligation.

Question 6: What else demands your attention besides ... <answer to question 4>?

In question 4, you have identified one problem, while in question 5 you challenged prospects to understand the seriousness of that problem. Now you challenge them to identify more problems. You continue to ask questions about those problems, and you can then ask why they require attention.

Question 7: Tell me about your interest in ... <the initial question>.

Finally, you ask prospects what they want to achieve. Ask them to explain why they wanted to talk to you. What are their aspirations? Where do they want to go? What does the world look like once their issues have been solved? Why does that matter?

"What do you expect from me?" can also be a good question. If you let the prospects think about what is needed to solve their problems, your offer will not come as a surprise. Asking "What do you expect from me?" instead of "What do you expect from a future accountant?" is also a powerful use of language. You're already planting a seed, making it sound like the collaboration is already a fait accompli.

That is much more powerful than the opposite version (which I often encounter): "What do you expect from someone you might work with?" Framing your questions and discussion in positive terms shapes clients' expectations.

To be able to make the right offer at the end of the conversation, you must listen on two levels. First of all, you listen to the content of your prospects' stories. You want to understand their situation as well as their problems and goals. At the same time, you must listen at the level of your offer. While listening, you evaluate your prospects.

You want to decide whether you want them as clients, and also what program you want to offer and for what price.

3. Answer questions

After you've asked prospects about their situation, problems and goals, you invite them to ask you questions. They may want to get to know you, and they may also have substantive questions. If the substantive questions are easy to answer, answer them! In doing so, you immediately provide value and that helps gain trust. If the questions are too complex to answer within a few minutes, be clear and explain that you would like to help them with those issues in the coming weeks. If they want to know immediately how you can help them further, it is a nice bridge to the next part of the consultative call.

4. Offer your services (or not)

Based on what has been discussed, you can make the prospect an offer or decide not to.

You make an offer

If it turns out that you are indeed speaking with your ideal client, you are now ready to present your offer. But before you do this, summarize what you have heard:

"You told me that ..."
"Currently, your biggest challenge is ..."
"Your goals are ..."

If your summary is correct, prospects will feel that you really understand them, which makes it easier for them to say yes to your offer. If your summary is incorrect or incomplete, prospects will interrupt or provide additional information. It is crucial that you listen carefully to what they say and then give a new summary. You can only make your offer after you have given a clear summary. The prospect will only work with you if you get things absolutely right. If that is the case, you can make your offer: "I'd love to help you with this. Shall I tell you what I'm thinking of?" or, "Do you want to know what possibilities I see?"

This is the moment when you tell your clients how you can help them. It's also your chance to show the client that you are the right man or woman for the job. You aren't giving a standard sales pitch. The challenge is to keep your pitch relevant to your clients. Don't tell them about your experience with investing if they already have an investment advisor whom they are happy with. Don't tell them that you mainly work in the Cloud, if the conversation has shown that they already understand. Don't tell them about your custom reporting package if the design of reports hasn't been discussed yet. In other words, tell your clients what they need to hear. Do tell them about your experience with their industry. Tell them that you are indeed working with the accounting package they already have experience with. Tell them that you can really help him solve their biggest problem and say once more what that problem is.

Pay particular attention to the results your collaboration will yield. Don't say, "I will update your books every day," but say, "You will always have real-time insight into your figures, so you can make the right decisions." Before you make the switch to the investment, summarize point-by-point what a client gains from working with you. For example: "I'd like to summarize what I can do for you ..."

- "You will always have real-time insight into your figures."
- "I will support you in making a profit plan."

- "With the aid of monthly coaching sessions, I will help you actually achieve your goals."

Then you ask:

- "Does this match your wishes and expectations?"

If the client answers this in the affirmative, the time has come to address the investment they will have to make: "Your investment for this is xxx per month." You give clients the opportunity to respond to your price. If they're not wholly happy with the offer, they may raise objections. An objection does not mean that you can't move forward. It may just mean that your prospect isn't yet convinced that you're a good match. I will explain later how you deal with objections.

You want to make an offer at a later stage

In the ideal situation, you decide which offer to make during the meeting. This obviously requires you to offer standard packages or programs. If you are unable to make an offer immediately during the meeting, you simply explain that you would like to make a tailor-made proposal. To prevent the process from stalling afterward, it is best to immediately agree on two things:

- when you send the proposal;
- when you call to discuss the proposal.

You do not make an offer

As soon as you notice that the prospect is not your ideal client, you can end the meeting with the words, "I'm not the right person to help you with this." You could even give a referral to someone in your network who you think might be a good match:

"I'd love to put you in touch with ... because I think he can help you further."

5. Finish

Ideally, there are three possible outcomes of the conversation:

1. There is a deal.

2. There is no deal.

3. A follow-up is needed.

1. Deal

Sometimes clients spontaneously say "yes" to your offer and sometimes you have to ask for that "yes". If clients accept your offer, then confirm their decision so you're both absolutely clear. Say, for example: "Thank you for your trust, I look forward to working with you." If the "yes" is not yet entirely clear, ask for it explicitly. Ask, for example: "Do we have a deal?" or, "What are you saying? Are we going to do this?"

After the deal, you tell the client what the next steps will be. These are:

– *Confirmation of Assignment* – Do NOT send an offer as follow-up to the consultative call. The client has already agreed to your proposal, so don't muddy the waters with another decision moment. Instead, send a Confirmation of Assignment, containing everything that has been discussed. Say, "This week, I will send you a Confirmation of Assignment with a copy of our General Terms and Conditions. I would appreciate it if you could sign it and return it to me within seven days."

– *Intake interview appointment* – Suggest looking in your calendars and planning the intake interview straightaway. As soon as you schedule a follow-up appointment, your collaboration has started. It also gives the client a lot of confidence if you take the lead in the next steps. This positive influence considerably reduces the possibility of the prospect withdrawing after all. I will explain this method of positive influence in more detail in section 10.1.

During the intake interview you will make a step-by-step plan for the practical matters that need to be arranged. Think of switching accounting software, getting access to the figures of the current year, and so on. You will also discuss the division of tasks and the processes. In section 8.1. I will discuss this intake interview in more detail.

2. No deal

Even when you do not come to an agreement it is important that you end the meeting on good terms. The prospect may not be a client now but can become one at a later stage.

Or prospects may know someone they would like to refer to you. You never know in advance what a conversation may lead to, so make sure you end it positively. Ask, for example, "Is there anything else I can do for you right now?" or say, "What I'm going to do now is ...' Thank prospects for their openness and wish them success.

3. Follow-up

Of course, you would prefer to come to a clear resolution on the spot, as following up requires additional time and effort. But you also have to be realistic. If you're asking for a considerable investment, you won't always be able to close the sale during the initial conversation. Some prospects may want to discuss your proposal with a business partner or simply mull it over.

If it turns out that there are no real objections, but your prospects just don't want to commit on the spot, make a clear follow-up appointment. Never end the conversation with, "I look forward to hearing from you." That is not fair to either party. You have both put a lot of time and energy into the consultative call and that deserves a careful conclusion. So make a concrete follow-up appointment. Say, for example, "I think that's very sensible. How much time do you need?" Or, "Shall I call you at 3 p.m. on Thursday?"

How to deal with objections

As soon as you have made your offer and ask for a "yes", objections can and will be raised. That is not a bad thing. This only means that prospects aren't yet confident enough to close the deal. Or perhaps your offer does not meet expectations. Don't let an objection discourage you. An objection is just an opportunity to get to the heart of a prospect's doubts.

The difficulty with objections is that they are not always expressed clearly. Prospects may find your proposal too extensive, but will say, "I think it's too expensive." Or they may say, "I first want to finish something else and I would like to start in a few months," while they're really not sure yet if you are the right person to help. As soon as they raise an objection, you should try to get to the heart of the matter. If you fall into the trap of responding to the content of an objection, there is a good chance that you will give irrelevant information.

I will cite several common objections:

"I want to think about it."

If prospects say they want time to think about it, this can mean two things: they genuinely need more time, or they don't want to say "no" and are making an excuse. That is why you always must ask more questions. Say "I think that's very wise," which demonstrates understanding. Continue with, "What is it exactly that you want to think about?" or, "Who do you want to discuss it with?" If they're concealing objections, it will now become apparent.

"I think it's too expensive."

As soon as you start asking higher prices, some prospects will tell you that they think it's too expensive. That is not strange. They may be used to paying $60, $90, or $120 per hour, so your proposal of $500, $1,500, or $2,500 per month doesn't fit their expectations. During the consultative call, you have gained insight into the problems prospects are struggling with and the costs of those problems. Remind prospective clients of these costs, both financial and stress related. Show understanding, remind them of their problem and ask, "I understand that it's a considerable investment. At the same time, you have just told me ... <prospect's biggest challenge>. My proposal will solve that problem. What makes you think the investment is too high?" You're encouraging prospects to link the investment to their problems and their costs.

If you have come to the core of the problem in the consultative call, and prospects realize that leaving the problem unresolved is more expensive than investing in your solution, they'll realize that the investment is not too high. They'll either say that you're right and they would like to work with you, or they will put forward a new objection.

"I can't afford it."

"I can't afford it," is a variation on "I think it's too expensive." But finding something too expensive is often an emotion. The price is not in line with expectations; prospects may be scared of the amount, but that says nothing about how much money they actually have. "I can't afford it" often says something about the actual balance of the bank account. It may well be that prospects don't currently have the means to pay you. At the same time, it is very likely that their problems will increase if they don't do business with you. Don't be afraid of discussing the risks you see and asking what they can pay. It often helps if you can suggest that they pay in installments. Sometimes it helps to think about how prospects can free up money to make this investment. Are there other costs they can reduce or get rid of?

"I would like to get an offer from someone else too."

If prospects indicate that they want another offer, they may not be convinced that you are the right fit for them. Why else would they invest time and energy to look further? In this case, ask for more information. "Why are you not yet fully convinced?" or, "What are you looking for in another offer?"

"Now is not the right time."

If prospects want to wait for the right time, they will never solve their problems. In fact, their problems will become even bigger. Bring reality into perspective by asking, "When will it be the right moment?" and "Isn't it true that there will be other things that will require your attention then?" Sometimes, it also helps to reflect on what life will be like if they don't take action now. I once literally said to a prospect: "Of course, you can also simply go bankrupt." That was the moment he decided to work with me.

There are, of course, countless other objections that a prospect can raise. The best way to respond to objections is almost always by asking an open question. Passionately seek out the core of the objection and remain detached from the outcome of the conversation. You will see that you happily and passionately convert the right prospects to clients.

Action step

- Draw your own sales funnel and determine, based on that funnel, what your first step will be in order to talk to more or better prospects.
- Create a marketing plan.
- Experiment with conducting a consultative call, so you can see for yourself what effect it can produce.

In this chapter, you learned how to talk to prospects and convert them into clients. Consultative selling places high demands on your communication skills. But you also need good communication skills to support your clients in acquiring new accounting habits, to coach them strategically with the help of the profit plan, and to work with Profit First.

In chapters 9 and 10 you will learn the finer points of powerful communication. In the next chapter, I will first discuss the question of how you can ensure that your clients will achieve results and feel satisfied with your support. The next chapter is about creating an unparalleled client experience.

8 CREATE AN UNRIVALLED CLIENT EXPERIENCE

* * *

Where focus goes energy flows - Tony Robbins

* * *

"And? How is Anne, your new client?" I asked Greg. Greg had been working with her for a few months when I spontaneously decided to give him a call. I was on the way back from an appointment and my thoughts turned to him.

Greg responded enthusiastically: "Great to hear from you! You know, what you are doing now, I just did with Anne last week. I had given her an assignment: she had to make an initial design for a better price structure based on calculation of the cost price. I was curious to see if she had already gotten around to it and if she managed to do it. So, I decided to call her. I had to get used to the idea, because we didn't have an appointment. But every time you call me, it makes me very happy. So, I just did it!"

"And? What did Anne say?" I asked.

"She said I was calling exactly at the right time. She didn't know how to proceed and gave up. My call helped her get her back on track so she could move on." He was silent for a while. And then Greg said, "I now understand what you meant when you said that offering value really isn't just about the number of hours you spend on the client. That conversation lasted less than ten minutes, but it prompted her to start using her new prices sooner. This conversation may have generated several thousand dollars!"

* * *

As a profit advisor, you must not let go until the client takes action. After all, you do not sell actions, but results. And for a good price too! It is important that from the very first moment, you and your client work together to ensure that those results are achieved.

Don't wait until clients act and upload their invoices. Your job is not only to process information and answer questions; your job is also to ensure that figures are accessible in real time, that there is a plan and your client focuses on profit. "Wait a moment," I hear you think, "I can't be responsible for everything! Clients must take action themselves. It's their company!" Certainly, you won't have to prepare your clients' sandwiches in the morning or turn on their computers, but your new role does require a considerable amount of proactivity and coaching from you. Your new role demands that you support clients in learning new accounting habits, that you remind them of deadlines you've set together and that you gently motivate them when they're ready to give up. You are coach, advisor and big stick, all at the same time.

You want your clients to get a return on their investment in you sooner rather than later, so it becomes evident you're worth the continuing investment. You want them to share their enthusiasm about you with people in their network, so that other ideal clients can easily find you. Finally, you want those results to be achieved as efficiently as possible, so that both you and your client will make a good profit.

What you need to achieve all this is trust, clear agreements, full attention and clarity about your role.

8.1 The intake interview

In 2004, I worked as an interim controller at a large international bank. I saw the bill of the accountant (belonging to the Big Four) for the month of September. The entry said, "various activities in September 2004," for an amount of $521,000, excluding sales tax. There was no further explanation or specification. I could hardly believe my eyes. Besides total amazement (what? how? what?), I also felt angry at the carelessness with which my client's money was handled, shocked at the ease with which hundreds of thousands of dollars were thrown around as if it were pennies. I called the accountant three-and-a-half seconds later to ask for a specification. Apart from really wanting to know what those five hundred and twenty-one thousand dollars had been spent on, it was also a matter of principle for me. I didn't think this is how one should conduct business.

I don't believe for a moment that you would handle your clients' money with such carelessness. But I cite this extreme example because it really helps to get my message across. Just adding up hours and sending an invoice at the end of the month with the description "work month..." No, that is no longer possible. And submitting the annual accounts "when they are finished," even when it is one-and-a-half years after the end of the fiscal year, does not meet the client's expectations. Now that you have a commitment to produce results and the client pays you a fixed amount per month for that, it is essential that you make clear, mutual agreements. You should both know who does what and when, and what you can expect from each other.

You must set aside time for this in the very first conversation you have as soon as a potential client becomes an actual client. Start your working relationship with clear goals and mutual agreements. At first it may feel as if you're taking too much time. But every minute you invest in a clear collaboration at this stage, you will soon earn back many times over. Simon Sinek describes this beautifully in his book *Start with Why*: "They never have the time or money to do it right the first time, but they always have the time and money to do it again."

Making these agreements is one thing, making sure they are implemented is another. Especially in the first few months, you will need extra time and energy to remind the client of the agreements you have made. Learning new habits doesn't happen without a struggle, but as soon as this form of cooperation becomes the status quo, it is a profitable situation for all parties.

The relationship between you and your client forms the basis of everything. How you deal with each other, what you think of each other, whether there is trust, what you expect from each other, what you ask each other to account for, which rules apply within the cooperation – all these factors contribute to the effectiveness and efficiency of the collaboration and, consequently, the results you achieve.

It is tempting to dive into the content immediately after the deal is closed. In the consultative call, you've probably gleaned plenty of useful information, and you may be ready to get started making your client more profitable right away. Holding an intake interview to discuss the relationship and the agreements can feel like a waste of time. But the intake interview could be the most profitable conversation you will have with your client in the coming period. In this conversation you lay the foundation of your cooperation; if all goes well, you will be building on this foundation for years to come. You will reflect on the mutual dependencies, tasks and responsibilities in the intake interview. Who does what and when? But also, what will the consequences be, in time and money, if one of you fails to stick to the agreements? You establish how documents will be shared, so that no time or energy will be wasted at any point. You agree on how and how often you will maintain contact. If you lay this foundation well, it will save all parties a lot of time, money and energy!

You should also realize that the intake interview informally determines the culture of your collaboration. By which unwritten rules do you deal with each other? If you talk about the kids and the upcoming summer holidays for more than half an hour in the first conversation, you set a different tone than if you immediately discuss the client's mission and vision. In this section, I write about the topics that should be discussed in the intake interview.

1. What is your "Why?"

In the consultative call, you discover which business your clients are in and what their biggest challenges are. If you really want to help, it's also important to know their motivation. Why do they do what they do? What is their mission? You want to get to know the people behind each company. You want to know what makes them tick, so you can minimize fallout when they do things that don't support their why, when there is a dip in sales, or when they lose focus.

In section 2.3, I discussed how to find your why. I suggest that in the intake interview you cover those questions with your clients. They can't be asked these questions often enough, because they connect their why to their actions. By paying attention to mission and purpose, you do justice to your role as a profit advisor. You indicate that it's not about debit or credit, but about much more essential things. This discussion will help raise the quality of the rest of the intake interview. You've set the tone: you're not talking about journal entries and general ledger accounts, but about making a profit.

2. Who does what?

You need complete clarity when it comes to who does what. Confusion of tasks and responsibilities is disastrous for efficiency and client satisfaction. Ideally, you map out responsibilities on the basis of a standard list containing the most important processes. You then create clarity in, among other things, the following areas:

- Who ensures that invoices and receipts are entered in the software?
- Who sends the sales invoices?
- Who processes the purchase invoices and receipts? Who matches the bank entries to the invoices?
- Who does credit management?
- Who pays the purchase invoices?
- Who files the sales tax returns?
- Who takes care of inventory management?

3. When?

The next question is about when the work will be carried out. Many processes are interdependent. You can only match the bank entries once the invoices have been processed. Your client can only do effective credit management after you have matched the payments to the invoices. You can only file the sales tax return effortlessly and without delay if the client ensures that all invoices are in the system on time. As soon as one of the parties fails to perform tasks on time, the whole system becomes a mess. You can't continue, emails will be exchanged, and frustrations will build up. That will immediately cost time, energy and money.

Some actions are best performed immediately. Think of scanning receipts: a receipt that disappears into a bag or drawer costs money. Teach your clients to scan receipts immediately, preferably while they're still in the store or even before they take the pizza out of the box. It is also best if the client forwards a purchase invoice to the accounting software immediately. This means that the invoice won't get lost among the hundreds of emails in an Inbox. In practice, sales invoices are usually sent once a month. It may help to talk to clients about the best time to send invoices. For example, if they regularly have cash flow problems, they would probably be better off switching to fortnightly billing. With such a relatively minor piece of advice, you can already become invaluable to your client.

Based on the list you drew up for the "Who does what?" section, determine when the most important actions will be carried out at this stage.

4. Exchanging data

From the moment you and your client work with the same cloud-based accounting software, a lot of data is exchanged in the most efficient way. Everyone works with the same software and it contains all relevant data. But in addition to invoices, receipts, bank statements, and sales tax returns, there is always more information that needs to be exchanged. For filing the income tax return, for example, a whole stack of data must suddenly be forwarded to you: pay slips of the spouse, mortgage statements and so on. It creates a lot of work for you when these are sent by email, especially when this information is spread over several emails, and those emails over several days or weeks. You are guaranteed to lose things, and your client will have to send information for the second or third time, which causes frustration.

I suggest that you look for a cloud-based system where your client would upload data into a shared folder so that you and your team can find it there. Various modern accounting systems allow you to store not just standard accounting documents but also other documents, such as contracts and tax assessments.

5. Accessibility

Your processes should be so clear that there will be no need to communicate about standard activities. In the ideal world, you never have to ask for a receipt again, and the client never has to ask if the figures are finished; the receipt is in the accounts and the figures are always updated up to yesterday or last week, whatever you have agreed. In the real world, however, there are always questions. Suddenly an overseas payment has to be done, or the client is considering buying another car and wants your advice. Maybe there's a complicated contract a client has questions about.

How do you want to deal with this? Are you always available? And would you prefer to be emailed? Or called? Or do you prefer to communicate via WhatsApp? Can your clients still call you after 5 p.m., or would you rather they didn't? How quickly can the client expect an answer? It is important that you think through your accessibility policies and communicate them clearly. Since I have discovered that I work much more focused in the morning than in the afternoon, I want to avoid being disturbed in the morning. That boosts my efficiency and the quality of my work as well as my profit. My clients and team members know that, and, therefore, rarely call me in the morning.

6. Consultation

How do your periodic meetings take place? At your office, at the client's office, or do you hold them online via a meeting tool such as Zoom or Skype? There are many options and it's important that you're clear from the start, so that there will be no wrong expectations or associated disappointments.

In this section, I gave practical guidance on how to streamline cooperation. In Chapter 11, I will go into more detail about setting up your own internal processes.

7. Issues that fall outside the scope of the agreements

Ideally, your agreement should cover all questions and problems the client may face. But there are, of course, exceptions. If, for example, the client unexpectedly decides to change the company's legal form or open a branch abroad, you should explain that this is not included in the current agreements. But if you just suddenly start invoicing for hours the client did not expect, the relationship will become strained. You must therefore already briefly discuss during the intake interview how you will deal with these situations. For example, indicate that you will never unexpectedly send an extra invoice, and that you will always notify clients in advance if work falls outside the agreed scope. In such cases, always provide a brief quote in advance. Transparency is essential when it comes to the costs of additional services.

8.2 Give attention

Attention is one of the basic necessities of life. Babies, partners, clients…even accountants: We all need attention. Many studies into why clients leave have shown that lack of attention is the most important reason.

Clients want attention. They want to be heard and feel that they are your most important, or even better, only client. My experience is that clients who feel like they get enough attention ultimately take less of your time. Clients to whom you regularly give attention feel the pressure to deliver on their commitments to you. They do their homework and prepare for appointments. That is the law of reciprocity. The scale must remain in balance, so the more attention you give, the more your clients feel inspired to hold up their end of the bargain. And that is where you ultimately want to go – because when clients do what you coach them to, your work becomes noticeably more fun, more effective and more profitable.

However, giving attention takes time – time that few of us have. The reality is that you can't afford to stare out of the window for half an hour on Monday morning thinking about why profits in José's business are falling. In the real world, the day is so packed that it does not even cross your mind to call Theo to check why he has not emailed the second version of his budget. In reality, there is no time to ask a colleague for his thoughts on the legal conflict in which Chiara is embroiled. In the real world, it is all too often that the client who shouts the loudest gets the most attention. Or worse, nobody gets attention because the sales tax returns must be filed this week.

I just tell it like it is: you must make time. You must organize your work in such a way that you create more time for clients. In Chapter 11, which is about systems, processes, and your team, I give you various organizational tips and advice on how to create time. In this section, I discuss the various forms of attention your client needs for an unparalleled client experience.

Make agreements about attention

Giving attention may have magical consequences, but there is really no magic at its core. Attention is just an essential part of your job. Without attention everything dies, which means you must make it a priority. Just as you plan to file all first quarter's sales tax returns by April 30, you must plan giving attention.

I have a client who needed extra attention before he took the step of actually uploading his receipts and invoices. After discussing the situation with him several times, I decided he needed a little push. I asked him to set aside a fixed hour every week when he would update his accounts. After some hesitation he decided on Mondays at 7:30 pm. As he is an important client to me, I promised him to call him every Monday for at least six weeks at 7:25 p.m. I put it in my diary and made it happen. Because he knew he could expect my phone call, he organized his own work better. In those few minutes on Mondays, I not only asked him what exactly he was going to do so I could interfere if necessary, but we were also able to immediately solve small problems.

If you feel reluctant to do this – "I can't go and call all my clients on Monday evening!" – you should realize two things:

1. You don't have to call all your clients. For most clients it's not necessary, and there are also several other options. Eve is a client who had considerable backlogs and needed to clear them. I could support her in the process, but she really had to take action herself. The high mountain of misery paralyzed her completely. We made a four-week action plan, so she knew exactly what to do and she could see the light at the end of the tunnel. I asked her to email me an update every Monday. She did; she went into action and emailed me. I read her messages and responded when necessary. And the one time she didn't email me, I reminded her.

2. *Your client has paid for it.* Of course, you can only give attention if your clients pay you for it – which does not mean that you invoice these calls separately. If your clients pay you well enough, these phone calls, emails, and contact moments are already included. *You do what it takes!*

Create time to give attention

Giving attention should not be at the bottom of your priority ladder. Attention and profit are alike in that way. If you wait until all your expenses are paid to take your profit, there's never anything left over. You must take your profit first. Likewise, if you don't give your clients attention until all your other tasks have been completed, you never find the time for giving that attention. The result is that your clients are dissatisfied, and you never achieve your own goals. Here are some practical tips based on my own experience:

Send welcome packs

I always welcome my new clients with a welcome pack. I send them a book, a pen, a bar of chocolate and a handwritten card. It is greatly appreciated! If you have not yet written a book, give new clients a business book you think contains valuable lessons. Enclose a card and explain why you chose this book. Ultimate attention!

Top five on top of mind

On the planning board in my office are the names of my top five clients. Every time I look at my planning board, I see their names and ask myself what I can do for them right now.

Call when you are in the car

When I am in my car, I make calls. Period. When my kids are with me, we listen to children's songs, but otherwise I call. If I don't have a call appointment, I go through my most important clients in my head, one by one. And then I call the ones who catch my attention. If I know they have a big project going on, I ask about it. Sometimes, I just ask how it's going and if there's anything I can do for them. And if I get his voicemail? Then I leave a very brief message, knowing that I still get those important brownie points for giving attention.

Take every opportunity to give attention

I recently received an email from a client in response to a payment reminder.

"Oh, how terrible of me, Femke," he wrote. "I paid your invoice immediately!"

I emailed him back, "Thanks for your payment, Philippe! How are you and your business doing? Is there anything I can do for you?"

Philippe is not one of my major clients. He follows an on-line program with support through a limited-access Facebook group and webinars. But that doesn't mean that I don't want Philippe to achieve results. I hadn't heard anything from him for a while, so when he was also lagging with the payment of the invoices, I started to worry. By giving him just that little bit of extra attention, I invited him to become active in the program. It only took me a minute and I received an immediate reply.

Communicate even when there is nothing to say

In the absence of information, clients start inventing their own story, which is rarely a positive development. If clients haven't heard from you for a while, they may think you have forgotten them! Even if clients are up to date, not dealing with any crises, and other clients are dominating your time, make time to check in. Send an update with information about the progress you see them making. Send a brief email asking him what they're working on and ask if they need help. If everything's running smoothly and there really is nothing to say, send a message to say that you are proud of them because everything is going so well now!

Create a culture in which agreements are binding

If you have just fallen in love, giving attention is easy. When my husband and I had just started seeing each other, he went on a skiing holiday with colleagues. As an expression of my love, I quietly slipped some mints wrapped in a note in his coat pocket. Last week he went skiing again. We have been together for ten years now, and there was no note in his coat pocket this time. Or any mints...

The first weeks of the relationship with a new client are like new love. Your new client is constantly on top of your mind, and when you're in the car on your way to an appointment, you call spontaneously, just to check if everything is going well. After six months, when the spell of new love is gone, you suddenly realize that you haven't been in touch for a month-and-a-half. But this isn't a client who pays you for your actions; this is a client with whom you have entered into a result commitment. Those few mints are not an option, but part of your agreement.

So, when I didn't hear from Eve, my client with the backlog, on the fourth Monday, I called her. If I hadn't done that, all the past effort would have been for nothing. She'd committed to emailing me every Monday, but without consequences for missing that email, that's an easy habit to break. You and your clients must hold one another accountable.

If you agree something, be prepared to stick to that agreement and send your clients reminders if they don't stick to their end of the bargain. In no time, you will have created a culture in which agreements are not optional, but binding. And that is when you're going to see results!

Automate giving attention

It sounds a bit contradictory, but even giving attention can be partly automated. If you file the sales tax return for your clients, send them an automatic quarterly email stating what actions you still expect from them so that you can file the return correctly and on time. It can be a standard email stating that they have until a certain date to update the accounts. Do you have a quarterly profit conversation with all your clients? Then send an automatic email with the request, preferably via an online calendar, to schedule the appointment. In February, send all your clients a checklist stating exactly what they need to submit so that you can file their income tax return. It is a one-off time investment for you, but it will give your clients a lot of added value.

8.3 The right role at the right time

Suppose an entrepreneur, let's call her Kim, is feeling stuck in her business. Things aren't going the way she wants them to. She is having to work too hard, and the profits are disappointing. Kim goes out for a beer with Jamila. Jamila says, "Make an appointment with your accountant." What do you think Kim says? She might say, "My accountant? Why should I ask my accountant for business advice?"

Kim thinks, just as many entrepreneurs, that accountants are there to book invoices and analyze figures. Figures on the left and on the right must balance, and then you calculate how much tax needs to be paid. Then what? Nothing. That's it. In Kim's perception, that is the whole story. That is what an accountant does.

Even if you have entrepreneurs who do share their concerns with you, they'll be less inclined to let you coach or advise them than if you were a business coach. These are missed opportunities. You have a wealth of knowledge about your clients' companies and about the effect that certain choices have on their profits. Because your clients, by their very nature, have blind spots when it comes to their company, there is a lot of room for growth. If clients were open to it, you would most likely be able to help them increase profits.

As a profit advisor, you will take on that advisory and coaching role. But this requires you to put on a different hat. You will learn in this section which hat that is and how to wear it.

According to Carl Gould, bestselling author, speaker, and entrepreneur expert, there are four disciplines, or four roles, which we take on as external specialists when supporting clients: consultant, advisor, mentor and coach:

1. *Consultant* – A consultant sees a problem, diagnoses it, and solves it. Consultants have expert level knowledge: they are IT specialists, lawyers, accountants, CPAs, and bookkeepers. Consultants focus on the technical side of the problem and fix it. They often have an impressive curriculum resume with a title (B.A., M.A., M.S.F., M.B.A., A.A., B.B.A.). They deliver impressive results, get articles published in a trade journal, or address an audience from a podium. A consultant is often the smartest person in the room.

2. *Advisor* – Advisors are generalists. Unlike specialists, they

don't know much about one specific field, but they do know a lot about many different subjects. They oversee the whole problem, can approach it from different angles and make connections. While advisors may direct the work of others, they will not actually complete the work themselves. Despite that, they're often the best paid people in the room. We pay advisors more money because they offer the right solution for many different issues.

3. *Mentor* – Mentors have gone through what you're experiencing, but they're several steps ahead of you. They take you by the hand and walk the same route with you, so that you can achieve the same results. They have specific knowledge of your industry.

4. *Coach* – Coaches facilitate you in your process. They help you get to the core of every problem but aren't emotionally connected to that problem and frequently set out a new problem-solving system, while letting you manage your problems yourself. They support you in your development as a person and entrepreneur, investigate with you what hinders you in achieving your goals and support you in tackling those obstacles. A coach pays attention to mindset and beliefs.

In the eyes of the entrepreneur, you have the role of consultant. The problem is that you may be seen as a subordinate by your clients. You do the work as they ask you to, just as an internal accountant does. You are paid for doing work, usually on an hourly basis. But your clients don't see you as someone who helps them take strategic steps and increase profits. If you want the role of advisor, with associated better pay, you must learn to manage your clients' expectations better. Don't sell yourself as an accountant who updates the accounts and takes care of the tax declaration, sell yourself as a profit advisor. Show your client what value you bring – value that your client will earn back in no time. And make sure you get paid as an advisor.

Of course, you still have tasks to do. The client's accounts still need to be done But why not have a team that takes care of those tasks? You are the advisor who helps the client make a profit. But beware: as soon as you roll up your sleeves as an advisor and start solving problems, you lose your role as advisor. The moment you start doing things – "Let me sort this out for you, I'll let you know next week what options are available to you" – you temporarily put on another hat, namely the consultant's hat. Be clear about and say: "I put on my other hat for a moment and, as an exception, I'll sort this out for you."

Action step

- Determine which topics you want to discuss during the intake interview. Record this in a document.
- Determine how you make giving attention an essential and non-negotiable part of supporting your client.
- Think about the different support roles and ask yourself which hat you wear the most, which hat or hats you want to wear more often and how you can incorporate that in your work.

This chapter was about creating an unrivalled client experience – by making clear agreements in the intake interview, giving attention, and making sure you put on the right hat. In the following two chapters we will further discuss the way of communicating with your client because communication is everything. What is relevant is not how much knowledge you have, but how much of it your clients understand and what they do with that knowledge. Communication is the link between your knowledge and your clients' results.

9 POWERFUL CLIENT COMMUNICATION

* * *

Successful people ask better questions and, as a result, they get better answers - Tony Robbins

* * *

Greg had just arrived for one of our last coaching sessions, during which we were going to discuss "complex conversations."

"Talking about complex conversations," Greg started, "What did you think when you first came to my office with Peter last year?"

"Do you really want to know?" I asked.

"Sure, tell me. I might learn something from it," said Greg.

"It is still fresh in my mind. Your first words said it all. You introduced yourself and said rather sharp, 'Why are you here?' That was not really inviting." I smiled at the memory.

"Yeah, that's right, I felt very threatened because Peter brought you along. As if I was being called to account," Greg said.

"I understood that," I said. "And with those few words, you made me feel like you were above me. And that I was the one who needed you, and not the other way around."

"Precisely," said Greg. "I wasn't aware of that then, but when I look back on it, that's exactly what I did. And you didn't oppose me. That helped. That made me feel less threatened."

"I seem to remember I thanked you for your time. And then I tried to remind you of the fact that we had a common interest: namely the financial health of Peter's company. But I must have hit a sensitive spot there, because you started to explain to me in detail and using a lot of fiscal jargon why the figures of the past year were not yet ready. I really had to bite my tongue then. I had at least a dozen questions, but I didn't want to get bogged down in the content; that is not why we came to see you."

"How would you avoid a situation like that?" Greg asked.

"I think I suggested that we step back a bit, so I could tell you why Peter decided to hire me and what my role would be."

"Yes, you did, that's how the conversation went." Greg looked relaxed. "It's a bit painful to look back, but it did teach me a thing or two. You were apparently very aware of how to approach me. I want to learn that too, because such a conversation could easily end in doors being slammed. I want to learn how to avoid that."

"Great! Let's get started!" It was a wonderful start of a valuable session about communication.

* * *

Communication is everything. You can be the very best in your field, but if the client doesn't understand you, it doesn't mean a thing. You can have the perfect solution, but if your client doesn't act on your advice, your solution has no value. You can believe you give it all, but if your clients feel like they aren't getting enough attention, you will have wasted lots of energy. It's never about what you say, know or are capable of, but always about how much of it clients understand and what they do with it. Communication is the link between your knowledge and their actions.

The most frequently heard complaints from entrepreneurs about their accountants are: "They don't communicate well. I don't understand them. I never hear from them." And I'll be blunt. Don't dismiss these statements by saying to yourself, "I'm not like that." I believe that the accountants who read this book are already miles ahead of their professional colleagues, including in the field of communication. And at the same time communication is a skill we all can improve. Everyone can become better at communication. Everyone.

When you take your communication skills to the next level, you will directly see improvement in what clients achieve, both in their results and also their satisfaction. Your profit margin and the enjoyment you get from your work are likely to increase, too. You may notice:

- Your relationship with clients improves. Clients are happier and will play a more active role during meetings. They ask better questions and apply the answers more effectively.
- Clients become more successful and more profitable because they're running their companies based on accurate, timely information and expert guidance.
- You spend less time on day-to-day bookkeeping and

chasing receipts. Instead, there will be more room for giving substantive advice, which will make your role more valuable.
- You then can easily sell your higher-priced consultancy services.

This chapter is about three essential ingredients that will help you tangibly improve the communication between you and your client. The first ingredient is the communication pyramid, in which the three layers of communication are discussed. Then we cover the three basic communication skills: Listening, Summarizing, and Asking Questions. Finally, you get practical tools for simplifying your communication.

9.1 The communication pyramid

The communication pyramid is an important model that shows why some conversations run smoothly and why others fail to achieve desired results. Understanding this model helps you intervene appropriately when a conversation is not effective.

Let me give you an example of an ineffective conversation. The client (C) is dissatisfied with his accountant's (A) services and requests a meeting.

C: "I'm not happy with how things are going now."

A: "What's not going well?"

C: "Well, several things. For example, I don't yet have any clarity about what the current situation is with raising my salary, which I recently emailed you about, and..."

A: "It's true that I hadn't responded to your email yet. I did look into it, but it took a little more time than I thought. I have also discussed it with a colleague. We both believe that it is not wise to raise your salary at the moment. The reason being..."

The accountant wants to keep the client and is eager to solve a specific issue. The client had asked a question about the possibility of raising his salary and did not receive an answer. The accountant tries to solve the problem by going into the details of one specific issue, the salary raise. Whether or not that particular issue gets resolved is not really relevant, because the client's dissatisfaction doesn't concern just that specific issue, but rather the cooperation in general. Even if the question around the raise is resolved, that dissatisfaction persists. What has gone wrong here? The accountant tries to solve the problem on the wrong level. The accountant focuses on the content, but the problem lies at a deeper level, namely, at the level of the relationship itself.

The communication pyramid (see Figure 5) provides a thorough analysis of the different levels at which communication takes place. Understanding the communication pyramid helps you approach a conversation in the right way or change the approach in time, so that the conversation will have the intended effect.

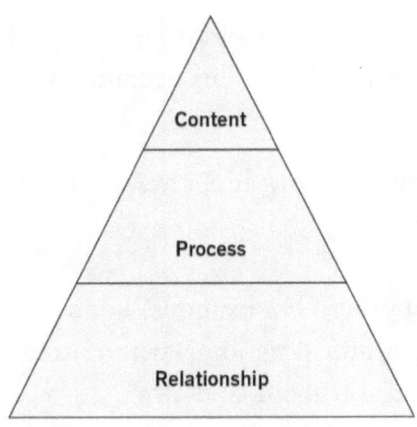

Figure 5: The communication pyramid

The communication levels that together form the

communication pyramid are relationship, process, and content. Any conversation is always conducted on all three levels simultaneously. In every form of communication – conversation, email, video chat – a message is communicated simultaneously at content level, process level, and relationship level.

Explanation per level

The *content*, which is at the top of the pyramid, concerns the facts, arguments, and opinions. The content is what the conversation partners usually come together for. There is an annual statement that needs to be discussed, the client wants to know if a company car would be a good idea, and so on. In Peter's example the content is that I, as an external advisor, want Peter's accounting process to be organized differently, so that he will have more insight into his figures.

The *process*, also called procedure, is the way in which the subject of the conversation is dealt with and how the conversation is organized. These are the rules of the game, such as who is in charge, what is the agenda, how much time is there? In Peter's example, the process was already a tricky issue. The appointment had been cancelled several times. I, as initiator, was in charge first, but Greg quickly took over when he asked why I came to his office.

At the pyramid's bottom level is the *relationship*, which regards how conversation partners deal with each other. How they see and hear each other, the atmosphere, the balance of power, and the emotions that conversation partners experience during a conversation – all this belongs to the relationship level. This level forms the foundation of every form of communication. Everything that plays a role at the relationship level has effects on the upper levels.

If you have just snapped at your husband (it happens to the best of us), then there is an issue at the relationship level. When you subsequently ask him if he will pass the cheese slicer (content), he might just reply with, "Get it yourself!" An issue at the relationship level always has a direct effect on the result you were aiming for. In this case, you still don't have the cheese slicer.

Intervening at the right level

If a conversation doesn't go well, most people naturally intervene at the top level: the content. They give another reason. They explain it again. They say it is "not true." If the problem really exists at this level, giving another reason is fine. Providing information is an excellent way to tackle problems at the content level. But very often the real issue is not at this level. The real issue is at a deeper level. And if you want to achieve your goal without wasting too much time, you should intervene at the right level.

This requires first that you understand the three levels of communication and that you then analyze at which level the issue exists. To be able to do the latter, it helps if you take a step back in difficult conversations. Look at the conversation or the email from a distance, with detachment, and try to establish which level of the communication pyramid plays the most important role. Then you intervene at that level.

You intervene at the content level by asking questions and giving information. In Peter's example, the real content was hardly discussed. There was too much noise at the process and relationship levels. This noise had to be removed first. There is no point in discussing the content if there is noise on the lower levels. The likelihood of Greg really listening and real results being achieved is non-existent in that case.

Intervening at the process level is done by aligning the agenda, letting someone else speak or agreeing on a deadline. In Peter's story, I intervened at the process level when I said, "Let's step back a bit."

Intervening at the relationship level is often the most challenging. You make it possible to discuss what is often not discussed in business communication: emotions and feelings. Once you talk about emotions and feelings or about the mutual relationship, it becomes personal. You introduce yourself into the conversation, and you invite your clients to open up as well. It turns out that you're doing more than just talking about a profit and loss statement or a lease contract. You're forging stronger bonds with clients, and you'll discover that if you give attention to the relationship level, the conversations about content become much more valuable. You create more value for your client, and your work will give you more satisfaction.

Intervening at the relationship level is done by creating space to discuss what is going on below the surface. You can observe what is happening and then present your observations, possibly supplemented with a question. You might say, "I notice that you're quiet. What's on your mind?" Or, "I think you're upset; am I right?" The first observation, "you're quiet," is more straightforward than the second one. Concluding that someone is upset is an interpretation based on other observations: raising one's voice, becoming red in the face or speaking faster. If you want to explore this in more depth, I recommend that you read more about non-violent communication. The effect of intervening at the relationship level is often that expression is given to what's really going on, which almost always makes it possible to gain more effect at the content level.

9.2 LSA as an essential skillset

LSA stands for Listening, Summarizing and Asking questions.

In my experience, these are the three basic skills in communication; if you master them, you are taking an important step toward high-level conversations that produce the desired results. When you truly understand your clients, the conversation becomes effective. By this I mean that the conversation achieves the intended result. Mastering these skills can make the difference between being a fine accountant or a profit advisor. If you apply these skills in the consultative call, they can easily help you double your income.

Listening is the most underestimated, the most complex, and the most important skill in the work of any advisor. Most frustrations in the relationships between accountants and clients arise from poor listening. Not understanding each other can have profoundly expensive results. Summarizing is also an essential skill for effective communication. Thanks to your summary, your clients will feel heard and understood. A good summary also reveals exactly what you have not yet understood. Finally, asking the right question at the right time is a skill that every advisor must master down to the last detail. Better questions generate better answers. Questions steer the conversation. They either bring you closer to the core or away from it.

LSA isn't a trick or a box you simply check off. It takes daily practice to master this skill, but the results are profound. It requires daily practice to master LSA, and even then, you can improve. On the other hand, LSA is simple and can be easily applied in practice. When I'm in a difficult conversation and don't know how to bring it to a good end, I remind myself of LSA. I will listen actively, summarize, ask questions, and take the conversation to a higher level, without exception.

Listening

Listening means hearing and trying to understand what the

other person says and intends to say, and showing in your reaction that you did. Listening is a lot harder than talking. When you talk, you get attention. And almost everyone loves attention. Listening requires concentration. The average person speaks about 225 words per minute, while we can hear 500 words per minute. So, we have about 275 words per minute "left", which we often use to think about other things.

Really listening starts with having a real interest in your conversation partners and in what they want to say. You enter the conversation with the intention of really hearing and understanding other people, really understanding where they want to go and what they encounter on the way to their goal. But we also have our own goal in that conversation. As soon as you are mainly focused on achieving your own goal in the conversation, you listen with the intention to react. If you manage to let go of that and listen with the intention to understand, then you are well on your way to becoming a Master of Communication.

We too often practice lousy listening:

- We don't really listen. Our thoughts are actually somewhere else.
- We pretend to listen. We look at the other person and make agreeing noises, but really want to start doing something else as soon as we get a chance.
- We listen selectively and hear only what we want to hear.
- We listen with the intention of reacting and make use of the first opportunity to react.
- We listen to form an opinion. We would like to give our opinion, our judgment, or our solution.

Every once in a while, we are all lousy listeners. But in conversations that matter, it is important that you listen purely and wholeheartedly.

Famous therapist Milton Erickson said that really listening requires that you put aside your own opinions, ideas, and what you think you know about the other. The first step is to have the intention to listen. When you intend to really hear and understand what the other person is saying or trying to say, you have overcome a major obstacle. The second step is to avoid the above-mentioned listening errors.

Pure listening

Observe yourself and others during conversations in the coming days and be alert to lousy listening:

- not listening;
- pretending to be listening;
- selective listening;
- listening to react;
- listening to give an opinion, judgment or solution.

By doing this regularly it will become easier and easier to spot your listening mistakes, so that you will start listening better and more purely.

Part of the definition of listening is hearing what the other person intends to say. That requires, besides having the intention to understand, something else, namely that you actively look for the message that the other person tries to convey. And in complex, tense or conflicting situations, that message is rarely contained in spoken words.

When Greg asked me, "Why are you here?" his words invited me to tell him what I needed. But beneath the surface, he also wanted to let me know, "I don't need this conversation." And, "I can't imagine that I'm going to like you at all." Greg probably still had a dozen or so unspoken messages for me. Because I did try to understand what Greg really wanted to say to me, I was able to respond adequately. What did I actually do to really hear and understand Greg? I did several things.

- I was aware of the setting in which this conversation took place. I had initiated the conversation. I was kind of an intruder.
- I did not take Greg's defensive attitude personally.
- I understood I needed to listen to the emotional level, rather than the content level of what he was saying.
- I put myself in Greg's position. I did my best to feel what he could possibly feel. I could do that because I have experience with similar situations. Therefore, my past experiences helped me react adequately in this situation.
- I not only listened to the words, but I also heard his intonation, I observed his body language and facial expression.

If you can purely listen, you are well on your way to actual understanding. What is pure listening?

- To have a sincere interest in the other.
- Not to judge or give your opinion.
- Not to give advice or try to solve anything. Listen.
- To stay with the other, not to think about what you're going to say or ask.

Real understanding usually does not stop with listening. Real understanding requires that you summarize and ask questions.

Summarizing

Summarizing or reflecting has the following important goals:

- The other feels heard and understood.
- You check if you really understood the other person.
- You reflect the structure and story of the conversation.

It is often recommended to summarize what has been said in your own words. That would be the best way to check if you actually understood. I recommend doing the opposite: to summarize in the words of the other. The other then feels really understood. Using your own words often has a counterproductive effect. Conversation partners may feel confused, because your summary isn't exactly what they said, which can lead to arguments about irrelevant details. Using the words of the other person has countless psychological advantages: they feel understood, they trust you, and they're more likely to accept your advice. That makes your work as an advisor much easier. If your summary is not entirely correct, the other party will let you know by interrupting you, giving you the opportunity to listen again.

Summarizing well is not that easy. A summary only needs to represent the core of what has just been said. As soon as the summary gets longer than the core, your conversation partner will become irritated: "Yes, I just said that!" A good summary therefore only consists of one or two sentences. If you summarize a long conversation, your summary can consist of a core key phrase and some bullet points. A summary is not only limited to the content, but the emotion, if it's relevant, must be included too. If Greg had gone to get an extra coffee after those first fifteen minutes, I could have looked at Peter and summarized it as follows: "That was a tough start. Greg feels threatened." That was an adequate summary, which captured both the core of the content and the emotion. A summary can, for example, start with:

"So, you ..."
"Do you mean ...?"
"If I understand it correctly ..."

Besides giving a complete summary, giving a reflection is also an important skill. A reflection can consist of just one or two words, often pronounced with an open end. You give the other person room to contradict your reflection. You use a reflection, for example, to show that you have understood the other person, but a reflection can also be useful if the other person wanders off and you want to bring him back to the core. If, for example, your client calls you up to complain about a tax declaration that seems to contain wrong information, and that he needs your help to rectify it, and before you can say a word he starts an emotional ramble about how this is the third time this has gone wrong and... You can smoothly steer him back on track to reflect the most important word: "And you need ..." Helping him to remember that he was the one who called you to get your help.

You can practice your skills by making one or two summaries or reflections during each conversation in the coming days. This practice can be in conversations with colleagues, but certainly also in conversation with your partner, friend or child. At first, these techniques may feel strange, but when you see that it has effects – that conversations become more pleasant and faster and that they achieve better results – you will very quickly start summarizing without thinking about it.

Asking questions

A third essential skill in powerful communication is asking the right question at the right time. When asking questions, it is vital that you realize you have the choice of which question you ask, and that the question you ask determines the answer you receive. When you ask, "What else?" it will bring new topics to the table. If you say, "Tell me," you will get more information about the same subject. If you ask, "What does that mean to you?" you will get information about how someone feels about it. If you ask, "Do you like that?" the answer is "yes" or "no," but you won't discover whether the person found it difficult or easy. Tony Robbins says: "Successful people ask better questions, and as a result, they get better answers." The challenge is therefore to ask the right question at the right time.

Asking the right questions requires you to keep an eye on what your goal is throughout the conversation. The question should help you move toward your goal, not away from it. It sounds like an open door, but just try paying attention when you are at a party or on the subway: most of the questions move the people asking them away from the core instead of toward to it. How about the conversation between two neighbors, one of whom, Karen, has just returned from a skiing holiday.

Karen: "There was an avalanche in the ski area, right in the area where our children were learning how to ski!" (The core of the conversation: she had a traumatic experience in which she feared for fifteen minutes that her children had been buried by the avalanche.)

Neighbor: "Oh, how awful, where were you then?" This question moves the conversation away from the core. A better question would have been: "Oh, how awful, what did you do then?" That gives Karen the opportunity to tell her story.

To be able to constantly move toward the core of the conversation, you need to pace the conversation. Take a moment to think before asking the next question. It is also important to make a conscious choice for an open or closed question. Do you want a quick "yes" or "no" or "left" or "right"? Then ask a closed question. Do you want new information? Then ask an open-ended question. An open question often starts with who, what, where, with what, when, why, or how. An example of an open question is:

"What exactly do you mean?"
"How do you see that?"
"Who would be suitable for that?"

Another way to get more information is by literally inviting the other person to provide more information:

"Tell me!"
"Can you tell me more?"
"Can you elaborate on that?"

An open question provides more information but has the disadvantage that it can lead to a long answer. Sometimes, interrupting your conversation partner is necessary to keep moving toward the core.

Interrupting

Interrupting your conversation partner halfway through a sentence is generally considered rude. However, I think it is an essential skill for successful profit advisors. People like to talk and be heard. We all get carried away by our enthusiasm sometimes. If, as an advisor, you do not interrupt your client, you waste time and money – both your own and your client's.

Interrupting your client is a very conscious activity. It requires you to be clear whether the client is sharing something crucial or not. If it's crucial, you don't interrupt, if it's not, you do. Topics can be intrinsically or emotionally crucial. Intrinsically crucial means that information is shared that must be shared so that you both can achieve your goal. Emotionally crucial means that, to the best of your judgment, your clients need to tell a story before they can pay attention to anything else. In all other cases you may interrupt. For example, if your client is telling you about a vacation in the Bahamas and starts a funny anecdote, feel free to say, "I'm happy to hear you've had such a wonderful vacation! Let's move on to...<*topic of conversation*>." Are you discussing your clients' accounting processes while they explain in detail why they're two months behind in scanning receipts? Interrupt away and ask, "What do you need to always be up-to-date with your bookkeeping?" This question moves the conversation back to the core, in this case, an up-to-date accounting system. The most important moment to interrupt is when a client is experiencing a moment of great insight. He might feel out of his depth and scare himself with fresh, bold ideas. His instinct might be to downplay this insight. He might make a joke or elaborate on a trivial detail. Please interrupt, and gently move your client back to the big insight he was sharing.

Ask the why question

The "why" question is a sensitive one. It depends a lot on your intonation, but "Why do you do that?" can make clients feel immediately defensive. However, I'm not always against the use of the "why" question. This question does help get into details, especially if you have strategic discussions with the client. "Why do you want to double your sales? Why do you want to expand your product portfolio?" The why question challenges the client to really think. In situations where the why question is really awkward, try reframing the question to make it a "what" question. "What made you do that?" often sounds less threatening than "Why did you do that?"

Continue asking question until you reach the core

The why question is often an important starting point to get the real story to the surface. However, it is usually not enough. After you've asked the why question, you can generally ask at least four more open questions that will take you closer and closer to the core:

Q: "Why do you want to double your sales?"
A: "So that my business will grow."
Q: "What will that produce?"
A: "More profit."
Q: "What does that bring you?"
A: "More income."
Q: "What will that give you?"
A: "Freedom."

Ah, freedom. It is essential to have this conversation with your clients. Because if you want to help your clients reach their real goal, freedom, they need your help during the journey. You know that more sales are often accompanied by more costs and/or more worries and/or higher taxes and/or more defaulters, and so on.

Do you want to steer your client in a certain direction? Then ask a steering question. I will discuss that in more detail in the next chapter.

9.3 The art (and necessity) of simplifying

Let's do a small experiment. Before you continue reading, I would like you to put your hand over this page so that you hide the next paragraph. Now I have a quick assignment for you.

Suppose that a start-up entrepreneur walks into your office. She has just graduated from a technical university. She is a smart lady but has never taken an economics course. She asks you: "Can you tell me what a balance sheet and a profit and loss account actually are?" What is your answer?

Answer to the question: "What is a balance sheet?"

Have you thought about how you would answer the beginner's question? And did your answer about the balance sheet contain one or more of the following words?

a. Debit, credit, assets, liabilities, fixed assets, current assets, equity capital;

b. Possessions, debt;

c. The balance sheet shows what a company is worth.

- If you score one or more words from option A, you are a real expert. You probably use much more technical jargon than you realize. Your client probably understands less than you think.
- Do you score words from option B? Then you are well on your way to using your client's language, but your client has to work harder than you realize to really understand you.
- Is your answer closest to option C? Then you probably followed one of my training courses ;-). This definition is far from complete and you might even say that it is not correct. But interestingly enough, it is the best definition, given the question I asked. I'll explain that in a moment, but first let's look at your answer to the second part of the question: "What is a profit-and-loss account?"

Maybe you'd like to review your answer first? Then put your hand again over the next paragraph. There I give my definition of the profit-and-loss account.

Answer to the question: "What is a profit and loss statement?"

a. One of three financial statements a company issues at the end of a period;

b. An overview revenue, costs and profit over a certain period;

c. A profit-and-loss account shows whether a company makes money.

- Is your answer the closest to option A? Then you use too much technical jargon. These words have little meaning for most entrepreneurs.
- Is your answer the closes to option B? Then you don't use complex words as such, but your client may lose track, because she can't immediately visualize your answer.
- Option C best fits your client's experience.

As a financial expert you have an enormous wealth of knowledge and you speak a language that your client only partly understands. Because you are that expert, you probably don't realize that you speak another language. For you, the words you use are normal. The point is: "Complexity is the enemy of execution." (Tony Robbins) The more complicated your explanation, the more difficult it is for your clients to follow and apply to their situation. Albert Einstein also said something clever about the use of difficult words: "If you can't explain it simply, you don't understand it well enough."

To ensure that the client really understands you, it is very important that you simplify what you want to say. Be aware that you speak a different language, a language the client does not understand. And because you don't realize that you speak another language, you also speak it fast. By the time your clients understand what you said in your first sentence, you're already on to your fifth. Then you've definitely lost them, right at the moment when you gave a valuable tip to increase their profit. A missed opportunity! Maybe you think I'm exaggerating a bit now. I'm afraid I am not.

Over the past ten years I have met and advised more than 10,000 entrepreneurs, and almost all of them have difficulty understanding their accountants. There are, of course, exceptions. But I'm not talking about those five clients now.

"If my client doesn't understand something, I'll just explain it again," may be another thought that comes to mind. Sounds very logical. Then your clients say, "Hey, I don't fully understand it," and you give an explanation. Problem solved, right? Well no, unfortunately not. Not wanting to be considered stupid or to prolong an already boring conversation (because it concerns figures from the past or something else they find irrelevant), clients will pretend they understand everything. They nod and hardly ask any questions. And after an hour, they leave dissatisfied. They feel like they've invested time and money but didn't get anything in return. The consequences are disastrous. The meetings are wasted money. Your valuable advice is not heard, and a simple question produces a very expensive answer, because it must be explained over and over again. The solution is as simple as it is complex: simplify.

Simplification tools

Fortunately, we have tools to keep our language simple.

Do not use jargon

Fixed assets, current assets, debit, credit, general ledger account, journal entry, equity capital, gross profit margin, solvency, suspense account, transit items, prepayments and accrued income, accruals and deferred income – this list is far from complete, but I'm sure you know where I'm heading. This is all professional jargon. To determine if something is jargon, just ask yourself if you regularly come across the term somewhere outside your office or business network. If the answer is "no", it is jargon. Be alert to its use and avoid it. Use words that everyone knows. To practice this, you can "translate" the following two terms: general ledger account and journal entry.

You can read my explanation below.

- General ledger account: a label that we assign to a cost category, so that we can group the various cost categories. This enables us to extract valuable reports from the accounting software. We can also gain insight into the various revenue categories thanks to general ledger accounts.
- Journal entry: a way of telling the accounting software where financial data should appear on the financial statements.

Understanding is more important than correctness

A big pitfall for financial experts is that they give an explanation that is completely correct. Yes, you read it correctly: it is a risk to give completely correct explanations. Finance is a complex field. So, if you want to give a complete and correct explanation, it quickly takes five to ten minutes or longer to explain. You then provide information that is of no use to your clients at that moment. They need to filter your full explanation to find the relevant information, the information they actually need and want. That takes a lot of energy, so they lose the thread of your explanation and give up.

It is up to you to choose to be less complete and correct. That's a big challenge, but always keep the goal of your conversation in mind. Your clients want to be able to make a choice or a decision. They don't always need to know all the fiscal rules. Sometimes you do need to talk about things in more detail so that a client can make a well-considered decision. In that case, use the following tool: first the big picture, then the details.

First the big picture, then the details.

Imagine a tree with lots of branches. The trunk is the question, and the branches are all facets, examples, and details of the answer. When your client asks you a question, you choose an approach for your answer: a branch of the tree.

Halfway through your answer you come across a side branch in your head: an addition to the answer you are giving, a further detailing, or an exception. You follow that side branch. Your client needs to switch gears, but he can still follow this detour. Then you come across a new side branch. You follow it. The client gets confused. Then you come across a third, fourth, and fifth branch, and finally a twig. But you realize that there is another branch that is also important for your answer. So, you follow that one too, including the corresponding side branches. The client has completely lost track.

Let me give you an example. Imagine your client asking you if it is wise to switch from a sole proprietorship to a corporation. A full answer could take three hours or even three days. I understand that. There are dozens of side branches to explore. An unstructured answer can start anywhere: the liability, the fiscal consequences, the wages of the director and major shareholder, the corporate structure, and on for paragraphs and pages. Let me share an example. An answer could be: "One of the biggest advantages of a corporation compared with a sole proprietorship is the difference in liability for the owner of a company. The owner of a sole proprietorship is 100% personally liable for the debts of the company. Except in the case of poor governance (1). This is the case, for example, when the entrepreneur has entered into obligations that the business cannot bear (2)."

In this example, a side branch is immediately explored: that of liability. At point 1, a turn is taken to an exception and at point 2, a turn to an example. Your clients can't see the big picture, the entire tree, and before they understand why the liability side branch is being explored and what the relevance is, you're already on the second twig. Clients can no longer follow the explanation. They're hopelessly lost. Too little attention was paid to the big picture and too much to the details.

Let's assume all the information you provide is correct. How can this still be improved? First give a brief and concise answer to the question – the main answer – even if that answer is incomplete.

If clients understand that main answer, tell them which other parts are also important. For instance, parts 1, 2, and 3 Then first explain part 1, check if the client understands it and continue with explaining part 2 and so on. Restrain yourself. Bite your tongue. Say less and stop earlier. And regularly check whether your client is still following you.

A structured answer, where we first explore the big picture and then dive into the details, could begin as follows: "The most important differences between a sole proprietorship and a corporation relate to liability and the fiscal consequences (1). I will briefly comment on both points. If you have a sole proprietorship, you and your company are legally one and the same. Company debts are also private debts. A corporation is legally separate. If your corporation incurs debts, you do not have to suffer from them privately (2). A second major difference is of a fiscal nature. Within a sole proprietorship you pay income tax and within a corporation you pay corporate tax. That has quite a few consequences.

As you can see, there are many details I am not mentioning in this second example. I don't mention the various income tax brackets, corporation tax rates, nor that a dividend tax applies in the case of profit distribution, and I also don't talk about the compulsory wages for directors and major shareholders and the dozens of exceptions. I have skipped all those side branches. That makes my answer incomplete, but I first give my client the big picture (1). When that is clear, I briefly explain the two main elements from the big picture (2 and 3). Then we can explore the details bit by bit; one detail at a time and starting with the most relevant one. The client decides what that is.

Ask yourself what the real question is

Because your clients aren't completely at home in their own accounting and figures, they don't always know what they really want to know. It may be that they're asking what the differences are between a sole proprietorship and a corporation, when they actually want to know if they pay less tax when by switching to a corporation. So, try not to answer immediately when a client asks something. Try to find out what they really want to know. Pro tip: That's usually not an overview of the rules and regulations. Usually, they're looking for what rules and regulations mean for them, specifically. Therefore, always ask for more information. Ask, "Why do you want to know this?" or interpret his question: "Do you want to know if switching to a corporation would be good for you?" Often an interpretation, if asked as a question, immediately provides a lot of clarity.

Connect with the client's experience

In everything you say, ask yourself whether it applies to the client and in what way. Suppose you discuss the profit-and-loss account with your client, Vincent, a coach. An entry in the account is "direct costs," while Vincent has hardly any direct costs. It is only a small amount, because he occasionally rents a coaching location. Vincent asks: "What are direct costs?" If you give him a full answer, you will be telling him too much. You give the definition of direct costs, explain the importance of the gross margin and maybe even give an example of a cake factory that has to buy sugar and flour. But Vincent has hardly any direct costs, so this knowledge adds little or nothing at that moment. So, it's better to link it to his situation and say: "In this case, it concerns the costs of the coaching location that you occasionally rent. See it as a breakdown of your costs." That is incomplete, but sufficient for him. Vincent still understands, and you can move on to more important parts of the profit-and-loss account... like the fact that he hardly makes a profit.

Use the "why-and-what-for" technique

As a financial expert you have a lot of knowledge of the "what". You possess a wealth of knowledge, and therefore it's logical for you to provide information. When you sit down with entrepreneurs, you undoubtedly tell them what you see: that their margin is falling, their solvency has entered a downward trend, that the doubtful debtors must be written off and so on. However, clients may question the relevance of the material you cover. They don't actually know what to do with the information you're sharing.

The challenge is not to dwell so much on the "what", but to pay more attention to the "why" and "what for". Don't waste time explaining what's happening in clients' books, but rather what the implications are for their company. Before you start talking, ask yourself the question: "Why is this interesting for my clients," and "Why am I telling him this?" Ask yourself what you want clients to do. When you have that figured out, you start talking and you first emphasize those things. You then say, for example, "You're earning less money with your company than before. What is the reason?" That is better than, "The margin is declining." A declining margin is purely technical information. Entrepreneurs, especially if they consider finances difficult and boring, will unconsciously shut their minds off to that information. They shrug their shoulders and wait for you to get to the important stuff. But if you frame the discussion in terms of having less money in the bank, then it's relevant! They'll be more open to talking about it with you.

Another example: "Solvency is decreasing" is quite factual and rational, but it has no meaning for the average entrepreneur. In real life, entrepreneurs don't talk about solvency. Say instead, "This year you have taken more out of the business than you earned. Shall we look at what a realistic salary is in relation to your current sales and costs?" Now you're talking about something that concerns them personally and profoundly. They won't like this subject, but they will find it relevant enough to want to know the details and take action. And that's what it's all about in the end.

Finally, the doubtful debtors that must be written off. This, too, has hardly any meaning for entrepreneurs. "Okay," or "whatever you say" are common reactions. They hear an accounting term, but don't understand the impact on daily decisions. But if you say, "The profit will be $20,000 less than you thought because client X will definitely not pay the invoice," then this suddenly has an impact. Then it is something that does lie within the frame of reference: profit.

Action step

In the coming weeks, be aware of the communication pyramid, LSA, and the extent to which you are simplifying. Discover for yourself what you are already doing, consciously or unconsciously, and what you need to pay more attention to. Also look back at a conversation afterward. Not to catch yourself making mistakes, but to discover what worked and what didn't, so you can try something else next time.

Communication is everything. That's how I started this chapter. You learned the basics of effective communication: communicating at the right level, LSA, and simplifying. You should use these skills in every conversation with your clients. The next chapter will discuss communication skills that you use when the circumstances demand it: influencing, coaching skills, and giving feedback.

10 COMMUNICATION SKILLS FOR SPECIFIC CHALLENGES

* * *

If you can speak, you can influence. If you can influence, you can change lives - Bob Brown

* * *

"I believe I understand it!" Greg went straight to the point. "Last time we talked about influencing, and I really resisted the whole concept, but it does work!"

"What happened?" I prompted Greg.

"Anne came to see me recently, and she told me that she'd had a pretty good month. And then she literally said: 'I think the good weather helped.'" Greg almost looked angry telling me this.

"Right, and that made you angry?" I asked.

"Yes, a little. Anne had worked very hard to achieve results but then she gave all the credit to the weather. I then remembered your lessons about influencing and I applied them quite deliberately."

"That sounds good. What did you do?" I asked.

"I first drew her attention to the mistake in her reasoning, and I said that she owed the results entirely to herself. And then I made an if-then statement. I said: 'Imagine what would happen if you maintained these qualities in the coming months and years. Just think of what your company would look like in a year's time if you kept planning, focusing, and managing the company based on your figures. If you can do this, Anne, then I can't wait to see what else you're going to accomplish.'"

"I'm speechless," I said.

"That's exactly what Anne said too," boomed Greg.

"And what exactly do you understand now?" I said, in a slightly more serious tone.

Greg considered my question a moment and then said: "By choosing my words consciously, I helped Anne to realize what she has been doing right. I am sure she is now even more motivated to keep up those practices that apparently work, such as planning and managing based on figures. And then she will achieve her goals."

* * *

The previous chapter dealt with essential basic communication skills. These skills will help you support your clients to the maximum and enable you to get more satisfaction out of your work and make more profit. You will spend the rest of your life honing these basic skills – communicating at the right level of the communication pyramid, listening, summarizing, asking questions, and simplifying. You will apply the basic skills in every conversation and in every email.

This chapter discusses three more skills that you use when the situation demands it: you want to achieve something in collaboration with the client, but it isn't happening automatically.

10.1 Influencing through language

Language is an extremely powerful tool. It can make or break a person. It can motivate, encourage, offend, enthuse, support, or seduce. You influence people with your words, whether you want to or not.

If a girl hears from her parents that girls can't do math and that men must provide for their families, these are just words. They say nothing about her ability to handle finances well. But if that girl later becomes an entrepreneur and she tells you that she isn't good with numbers, you will probably accept that as truth. Imagine that your client discovers after several years that most entrepreneurs are using advanced, entrepreneur-friendly software to do the books themselves. She tells you that she would also like to learn this. Suppose you say: "Do you think you should? After all, you're not very good with numbers." That would make her feel unsure of herself. If she still decides to go ahead with it, she will be afraid to make mistakes and her very first mistake will confirm for her that she really can't do it.

But if you say to your client: "I think that's a great idea, you're clever enough and you're a fast learner." It is then very likely that she'll start in good spirits and discover that the whole thing is not that complicated at all.

Those are just words. But the words you choose have an

enormous impact on the self-confidence and results of your clients.

More than fifteen years ago, I completed my NLP Master Practitioner Certification Training. I always refer to NLP as a broad set of coaching skills as well as a very effective way of communicating. The way I communicate is largely shaped by everything I learned during my NLP training. I apply NLP daily without even thinking about it. This training taught me, among other things, important lessons about influencing.

We continuously influence other people. One of NLP's presuppositions is: If you influence anyway, then you better do it consciously. NLP uses the Milton model of language patterns for this purpose. The Milton model is based on the successful work of American psychiatrist and psychotherapist Milton Erickson.

The Milton model is a form of hypnotic communication and relies on a number of patterns that will enable you to influence clients in a positive way. Let's look at some of the most important patterns here:

- mind-reading
- cause and effect
- presuppositions
- suggestion of choice
- using quotes

Mind-reading

You claim to know the thoughts of another with the aim of making them believe it themselves. You say, for example: "It makes me very happy to see you starting to enjoy finance more and more." Whether true or not, putting this notion out there increases the likelihood of your clients beginning to have a more positive attitude toward finances. Think about the opposite: "I know you hate finance." Again, we don't know whether that's true or not, but odds are pretty good clients will agree and dread doing their bookkeeping work.

Cause and effect

This pattern implies that one thing leads to another, which leads the client to believe that it indeed is possible to achieve the other. You posit "if-then" statements. "If you do the accounts yourself, then you can also submit the sales tax return yourself." You put the client on a positive track of thought: "Ah, if I can do the one, I can do the other too!" A positive attitude makes it much easier for clients to take the steps you recommend.

Presuppositions

You make a presupposition that is not proven, but that helps clients reach the desired effect: "You're going to make better and more profitable choices if your accounting is always up-to-date."

Suggestion of choice

After learning the hard way, many parents make use of this language pattern. Telling small children what to do is often counterproductive. When I tell my four-year-old son to put on his coat, he will walk out into the snow in short-sleeves (true story!) My son wants to make his own choices. If I want to suggest a choice to him, I will say, for example: "Are you going to put on your coat yourself, or shall I help you?" We're not discussing my underlying goal: getting him into that coat. Because the choice is expressed as a suggestion, my son doesn't perceive it as an order.

You can also apply this language pattern when working with clients. If your client continues to struggle to update his accounting weekly, you will probably encounter resistance when you say, "You must choose a fixed accounting moment." It might just work better if you ask, "Do you prefer to update your accounts in the morning, for example every Tuesday at 9 a.m., or would it work better for you to do this in the afternoon, for example every Thursday at 3 p.m.?" It's a given that the accounting takes place each week, and now you're just sorting out the details.

Use quotes to make something clear

Sometimes you must give a difficult message. You sometimes need to tell clients they've done something stupid, but you know that being blunt is likely to offend them. It may then help to have someone else – an unknown and absent third party – deliver the bad news. For example, "I recently read an article saying that people are much sharper in the morning than in the afternoon. I then wondered if it would be easier for my clients to do their accounting in the morning." Or if clients keep insisting that working with the Profit First cash flow management system doesn't work, while they're also saying they still lie awake at night worrying about money, you might prefer to quote someone instead of giving advice of criticism: "This reminds me of a famous quote, attributed to many people including Mark Twain, Albert Einstein, and Henry Ford: 'If you always do what you've always done, you'll always get what you've always got.'"

How do you apply the Milton model in practice? First, it is important that you should not see influence as unethical behavior, but as something that happens naturally. It's better to let it work for you rather than against you. It's also important that you use influence ethically. You shouldn't use influence to make people do things they don't really want to do, but rather to give them a helping hand in doing things they really want to do but don't dare or can't do yet. If it's helpful, think of influencing as encouraging.

I use the Milton model frequently, especially to motivate clients or participants in my training courses, to give them the feeling that they can do it, to empower them. I know that the way they think about themselves has an immense impact on the way they run their businesses, and therefore on their happiness and success. I make small successes bigger and confirm clients' ability to do what they already can do without even realizing they can do it.

10.2 Coaching questions

Coaching skills are essential in working with clients. You use coaching skills to help your clients take steps in their development, steps they might not have taken without your help. Obviously, reading this book, this paragraph, doesn't make you a coach. What I want to share with you are some essential coaching questions that you can ask in many situations and that will help your client quickly:

1. *What is your goal?* – This question has many variants. "What do you want to achieve next year?" "How much profit do you want to make this year?" "Where do you want to be in 10 years from now?" "What do you want to have achieved by the end of this conversation?" Whatever variant of this question you ask, you challenge clients to think about where they want to go. Any answer about goals, especially if it is a larger goal, often prompts more questions. "Why is this important to you?" "What does it mean to you if you achieve this goal?" Do not start too soon with asking your clients about the "how". Therefore, don't ask right away: "How are you going to achieve that?" The how question often immediately introduces obstacles, whereas it is very important to first understand what your clients want.

2. *What is stopping you?* – As soon as your clients fail to get something they really want, you could immediately offer a solution, but asking why he failed often leads to better outcomes. The clients then discover their obstacles for themselves, the first step toward the solution. Variants of this question are "Why is it not working?" "What stands in your way?" "What is the main reason?" "Why haven't you managed this yet?" This last question also includes Milton's language. By using "yet", you suggest that it will eventually work, and that can have a powerful effect.

3. *What is the solution?* – In addition to the previous question, it is also better to ask clients what the solution is, rather than suggesting the solution to them. Here too, the question makes your client think, and that is much more powerful than accepting your solution. A self-conceived solution is much easier to accept and gets implemented much earlier than a solution that has come from outside. Clients feel ownership of the solution when they devise it. Variants of this question are: "How do you think you can solve that?" "What is the best way?" "How do you find that out?"

4. *How can I help you?* – Another important question is about your role in your clients' business. Over the course of your relationship, you may ask this question several different times. Achieving goals, spending less time on accounting, having more insight into the financial state of affairs, getting paid earlier by clients, switching from a sole proprietorship to a corporation... these are all good reasons to ask, "How can I help you with that?" "What do you expect from me?" "How can I contribute to this?"

Instead of asking, "How can I help you?" experts often answer the question that's in their head but hasn't been articulated. They say, for example: 'I can prepare those financial statements for you," "I'll email you a step-by-step plan." "Get in touch with..." Coming up with a solution quickly often feels like an efficient step, but you may not actually be offering the best solution to the problem. Exploring and understanding a problem may take a little more time, but it's worth it. The second disadvantage is that your idea is your idea. A solution is much more powerful clients come up with it themselves. Involving your clients in developing solutions means they're more likely to follow through and act.

5. *What's bothering you?* – Sometimes, you just feel that something is bothering your clients. They may be unusually quiet or distracted, but they're not exactly forthcoming about what's on their mind. Just ask the question. Problems that are only in your clients' minds can't be solved. Get them out in the open. You can use the following ways to get your client to discuss them: "What makes you say that?" "What is bothering you?" "What's going on?" "What are you thinking?"

This is probably the most difficult category for experts: asking about feelings. As an accountant, bookkeeper, CPA or expert in another field, you may think this isn't your line of business. After all, you are not a psychologist, you are a number-cruncher – you deal with rational things. Chances are that this category of questions lies far beyond your comfort zone. Still, I want to challenge you to experiment with it. The point is that your clients are people of flesh and blood, with a whole host of feelings. And these feelings direct them in everything they do or choose not to do. These feelings affect success or failure. Asking about feelings can clarify many things and remove considerable obstacles.

10.3 Feedback

Clients make mistakes, they don't stick to agreements, a problem unexpectedly arises: These are all moments when you want to give feedback. Feedback is usually focused on the behavior of the other person, how you experience it, and how you would like it to change. That makes feedback both important and difficult. You don't like something, and you want to change it. That's a pretty big challenge. It's common to fear that our clients won't like us if we criticize them. Yet, it is precisely the lack of feedback that really causes problems. If you give too little constructive feedback, problems persist. Clients continue to send information at the last moment. They claim items that cannot be justified on business grounds, even after you have indicated that they are not business expenses, or they regularly arrive late for appointments. How can you give feedback in such a way that the other person will accept your feedback and that there will be real room for improvement?

I will first present a concrete feedback method. After that, I will briefly talk about receiving feedback.

SEED model

The SEED model stands for: Situation, Emotion, Effect, and Desired. These are the four steps you go through when you give your feedback. The SEED model is especially suitable for situations that go further than just matters of content, situations where the behavior of the other person causes you problems.

Imagine the following situation: you have a newish client who lets his administration run wild. He is months behind with uploading invoices and receipts. Also, some very practical questions you have asked are still unanswered. You have called him, emailed him, and talked to him about it, but to no avail.

You feel quite disappointed, because you were really enthusiastic about working with him. He has a fast-growing company and you were looking forward to supporting him in achieving a financially healthy and profitable growth. But very little of all your plans has come to fruition. Without figures, contact, or answers there isn't much you can do. You are having a meeting with him at your office.

As soon as he sits down, he starts talking. "I'm not very happy," he says. "I pay you more than my previous bookkeeper, but I don't yet see any added value. I still don't know how my company is doing, and I just don't feel that I have any insight into my figures. The sales keep growing, but I don't have any more money left."

Your heart rate accelerates immediately. You feel hot and you would rather just leave and slam the door on your way out. Yet you don't. You listen, summarize and give feedback according to the SEED model.

"You aren't happy because you don't see the added value of my services (*Summary*). I can imagine that you feel dissatisfied. I am also not happy with how things are going now. It really frustrates me that we are in this situation (*Emotion*). The point is that I do not have the information (*Situation*) to provide you with sound advice (*Effect*). Despite my repeated requests, I do not have all the documents or answers to my questions (*Situation*). I want nothing more than to support you in building a financially healthy and profitable company. That is why it is important that you also carry out your tasks. Shall we take another good look at the division of tasks: who does what and when? (*Desired*)."

As you can see in the above example, I'm using the elements of the SEED model, but they're not necessarily in a rigid order. That's usually how it occurs in reality. Let's analyze the individual parts:

- *Situation* – It is essential that you state the facts. What has happened? What has someone said? The challenge is to present the pure facts. Leave your emotion out at this point and certainly don't condemn the other. Do not say, "Great story. How on earth can I make reports if you are too lazy to scan invoices?" This answer is packed with emotion, and you are also insulting your client. That can, of course, lead to an argument. Separate the emotion from the facts and make no value judgement about the other person: "The point is that I don't have the information. Despite my repeated requests, I do not have all the documents or answers to my questions."

- *Emotion* – There is room for expressing your feelings in the SEED model. You are a human being of flesh and blood, and if there is no room for expressing your feelings, some things will be left unsaid, which can have a negative effect on the relationship. Do not vent your frustration. Do not judge your client by telling him he's lazy but tell him how the situation makes you feel. "I can imagine that you feel dissatisfied. I am also not happy with how things are going now. It really frustrates me that we are in this situation."
- *Effect* – Tell him what the negative consequence of the situation is. You client's failure to provide you with accurate and timely information means you are hindered in your effort to use your expertise to improve his profitability.
- *Desired* – Tell him what you think the solution is. If you don't propose a solution, the feedback won't be complete. Simply exchanging facts and emotion isn't enough. You may begin to understand each other better, but nothing will change. "I want nothing more than to support you in building a financially healthy and profitable company. That is why it is important that you also carry out your tasks. Shall we take another

good look at the division of tasks: who does what and when?"

The reason that feedback according to the SEED model works very well is that you separate facts and emotions, without ignoring either. As soon as something becomes an issue, everything (the situation, the consequences, and your emotion) may come out in one big eruption: "That is all your own fault, you lazy bum!" Venting your frustration in anger might feel good for a moment, but it won't solve the problem.

You don't give SEED feedback just off the top of your head, especially not the first few times. This is feedback you must prepare. Take a sheet of paper, place the four letters one under another and write down the corresponding information for each letter. You will notice that just listing the various components of the situation helps you control your emotions.

Receiving feedback

Receiving feedback is probably as difficult as giving feedback. Someone is criticizing you! Let's be honest; no one likes to be criticized. You will find that knowing how to receive feedback in the right way makes you a very powerful advisor. The ability to listen to and accept criticism, and to respond to it in a mature way evokes respect.

A natural reaction to criticism is to become defensive. "That's not true!" or, "Yes, but that's because..." Both alternatives are counterproductive. If you can't listen to feedback, other people don't feel heard. They'll push back, and then you have a conflict.

Look at this example:

Man: "You're a slob! Why do you always make such a chaos of the kitchen?"

Woman: "I don't! When was the last time you emptied the trash can?"
Man: "Yes, you do! The counter is covered in at least eight drinking glasses you use every day!"
Woman: ... (Well, you understand where this is going.)

The first point is: the feedback that the man gives does not follow the rules. But that's how it goes in real life: emotions and facts are intertwined, and we're quick to judge. But the woman in this example is not good in receiving the feedback either. She immediately becomes defensive and pushes back. The man doesn't feel heard and adds another serving.

How could the woman have reacted differently? Ideally, she would be open to her partner's feedback and accept it. She would say: "True, it is indeed rather messy in the kitchen. I haven't really cleaned up my mess today." That would then be the end of it.

Rules for receiving feedback:

- *Listen* – Listen to what other people say and mean to say and show that you've heard it. Thank them for the feedback if it is justified. Do not become defensive. Feedback can sometimes sound rough, but the other person probably also feels uncomfortable giving it. Your partners in discussions are trying to raise important issues, so try to hear their intentions. What is bothering them?
- *Ask questions* – Ask for an explanation if something is not clear to you. Ask more questions. Try to understand what's really going on.
- *Accept it, or not* – Decide whether or not this feedback requires action from you. The choice is yours. You also

need to decide whether it is necessary to tell the feedback provider what you have chosen to do about the feedback. "Thank you for your feedback, but I'm not going to do anything with it," means that you still want to have the last word. You pour some extra oil on the fire, which may not be the wisest move if conflict resolution is your goal.

To conclude this section, I will give another example of a good way to receive feedback. A client is in the process of switching from a sole proprietorship to a corporation. You support her in that process. She calls you and says: "Do you have a moment? I'm considering getting help from somebody else. I am getting more and more confused. I just don't understand you." A good reaction could sound like this: "Oh, I'm a little shocked by what you are saying. It is not my intention to confuse you more. What makes it difficult for you to understand me?" The client feels heard and the lines are open. There is a reasonable chance that this issue can be solved, and that the client will stay.

Action step

Thanks to the action step at the end of the previous chapter, if all goes well, you will become more aware of your conversations. You notice what works and what doesn't, and you can experiment with the various tools. Now add the tools from this chapter to the tools from the previous chapter. See where you can consciously influence, ask coaching questions, and if you need to give feedback, prepare it by using the SEED model.

This chapter deals with communication skills that you use when the circumstances demand them: influencing, coaching questions, and feedback. The next chapter is about your company, about how you design your company so it will run without you.

11 YOUR COMPANY AS A WELL-OILED MACHINE

Successful entrepreneurs design their business to run without them. – Mike Michalowicz

When I arrived at the office there was a letter on my desk with a foreign stamp on it.

Dear Femke,

Thank you, also on behalf of my wife. We are in Spain and I don't have a laptop with me. Otherwise I would have just emailed you ;-)

Before I became a profit advisor, I would not leave home without a laptop for half a day. I was always working, and I always felt guilty toward my wife and children. Every weekend, every holiday, my head was filled with a thousand and one loose ends, night and day. The client who had not provided any figures for months and now urgently needed annual accounts for a financing application. The 167 mails in my Inbox that required my attention. Questions from employees, clients, and suppliers. My bank account, which already for weeks had a worryingly low balance.

And then Peter suddenly showed up with you, because he didn't understand his figures. That was the last straw. It was really a wake-up call. In the weeks that followed, I started looking at myself and my company with different eyes. I suddenly saw that the image I presented to the world, that of a successful entrepreneur, free of the horrors of having a boss, free to make his own choices and, moreover, could put every dollar he earned in his own pocket, was no more than that: an image. The reality was distressing. I worked more hours in a week than I ever worked when I was still an employee. I was controlled by the endless stream of emails from clients. I had to work even harder than ever before, but now not only in my profession, but I was also flooded with all kinds of additional things: from marketing and acquisition to contract management, from my own accounting and payroll administration to website management. It just didn't stop.

It had been a long time since I had actually enjoyed my work, my income was variable and was sometimes even lower than the very first salary I earned after graduating, and when you and Peter came to see me, I realized that I did not even deliver the quality I advocated. It gave me a stomachache, but it also prompted me to act. I asked myself several fundamental questions:

Why do I actually want to run a business? What do I really want? For myself, but also for my clients? How do I distinguish myself from other accounting firms? How am I going to deliver results without working myself to death? And finally: "How do I free myself from the daily worries, so that I can work on my company instead of in it?" It has not been an easy time. But now I have been without a laptop in Spain for two weeks.

And this afternoon I went to a small Spanish village with my son to buy a stamp in a local shop.

Adios, Greg

* * *

You know who your ideal clients are, what problems they face, and you have a unique, proven and effective method with which you can contribute to the solution of that problem. You take on your role and ask the right questions. You are paid for the value you deliver, not for the number of hours you work.

Congratulations: you are a profit advisor!

There is one more thing... You want that solution to be delivered as efficiently as possible. And that delivery should not completely depend on your hands-on time and energy. You want your company to be able to deliver the solution.

11.1 What is a company?

We start with a definition. I understand a company to mean: *a driven organization which helps solve the client's problem as efficiently as possible.* Many entrepreneurs, possibly you as well, start their business from a passion (they like something very much), mission (they want to contribute to the world), or quality (they can do something very well). Even though all these things are essential ingredients, they are not enough to run a successful business.

Many financial specialists who own a company have made the mistake of thinking that mastering the technical side of the work (being an AA, ACCA, CPA, etc.) is enough to start their own business. But nothing could be further from the truth; that you are a good accountant says nothing about your qualities as a leader, nor does it mean that you have the right knowledge and skills to run a business. The result is that some accountants who start a company discover after a while that what they essentially have is not a company but a badly paid job with a lousy boss (themselves) where they have to work ridiculously long hours and bear a lot of risk.

Both accountants and their clients face the same struggle. You, the accountant, need to adapt to changing technology, offer more valuable services, and find a way to ensure that you don't have to personally handle every aspect of your business. Likewise, your clients need more than an accountant. They need a profit advisor. This chapter gives you the tools you need to transform your accounting practice into a machine that earns money even if you're occupied elsewhere. And as you learn this process for your business, you'll be learning how to help your clients become better, more secure entrepreneurs with more freedom as well.

Think about it. For both you and your clients, when you're on holiday, you're probably not earning any money. If you get sick, your company is in trouble, and if you die, that's the end of your business. The entrepreneur is the company. The entrepreneurial dream (more freedom, more time, more money) turns out to be a farce...until now. The rest of this chapter gives you the tools to build your company to make money while you sleep and lets you reach more clients to help them transform their own companies. While I'm addressing you – financial experts and profit advisors – keep in mind that many of the strategies you'll learn in this chapter can also apply to your clients' businesses as well as your own.

My definition of a company, a driven, profitable organization which sells a solution to solve the client's problem and delivers this solution as efficiently as possible, contains nine important elements. I will discuss them one by one, in a slightly different order:

1. *Driven* – The organization must be a driven one. By this I mean that it works based on a clear mission and vision, the drive of the organization. An organization that has this drive inspires, directs, makes choices, and achieves great goals. An organization that is not driven by a clear mission and vision is an empty set of actions. In the end, no one will benefit from it.

2. *Profitable* – Without profit there is no sustainable company.

3. *Organization* – The organization must solve the problem, not you or your team members as individuals, but an entity consisting of people, systems, and processes. Thanks to the organization, the results that your company achieves are not dependent on you as an entrepreneur. If there is no organization, there is no company.

4. *Problem* –There must be a clear problem, a problem that your clients need a solution for. Once you know how to solve that problem in an efficient way, you add value and you have the basis for a profitable business.

5. *Client* – There must be an ideal client with the problem you want to solve. The better you know those ideal clients, the easier you can find them and the better you can sell your product.

6. *Solution* – When you know what problems your ideal clients have, you can come up with a solution. At first glance, most accountants do have a solution to their clients' problem. They offer accounting services, draw up annual accounts, and do the payroll administration. But only if you offer the solution better, faster, cheaper, or in another distinctive way, will you have a company with potential. You could open multiple branches of such a company if you wanted to. Such a company is marketable,

because it has value that goes beyond your individual qualities and knowledge.

7. *Sell* – The solution to the problem must be sold before it can be delivered. This means there must be a strong marketing and sales strategy.

8. *Deliver* – Only after the solution is delivered, the entrepreneur has finished his side of the deal. Quality and client satisfaction are important elements where it concerns delivery.

9. *Efficient* – We also want to solve the problem as efficiently as possible. Efficient means that the problem is solved with an optimal use of resources like time and money, because that is the key to making a profit.

This chapter provides you with the essential ingredients to turn your company into a well-oiled machine: 1) goals, strategy & plan; 2) processes; 3) systems and automation; and 4) team. When all of these are in place, your company will not depend solely on your commitment or presence. Your company will solve problems, create value, and generate sales, even when you're not there.

11.2 Goals, strategy & plan

A big problem for many entrepreneurs is that they are swayed by the issues of the day. They come to the office, open their laptop, and work from their Inbox. They let the outside world decide when to do what and for whom. If Client A needs something, they start to work for Client A.

If Client B appears to want something that has not been delivered before, it is an opportunity to make money, so a product is developed especially for Client B. The company ambles from left to right and is not concerned with setting out its own vision, but mainly with satisfying the wishes of third parties. Unfortunately, it often takes a long time before the entrepreneur discovers that this is a problem, because it is quite possible to earn enough money in this way, sometimes for years. But sooner or later, entrepreneurs who just go to work every day and fail to focus on the bigger picture find themselves facing a wall. The team loses motivation, the owner loses motivation, clients are dissatisfied, and they may even run away.

Instead of being swayed by the issues of the day, as an entrepreneur you have the responsibility to set clear goals and a good strategy based on your mission and vision. We already discussed the mission and vision in Chapter 2.

Long-term goal

Ask yourself the question: based on my mission and vision, where do I want to be in five, ten, fifteen years' time? What do I want to have achieved by then? Related questions include:

- Who is my ideal client?
- What is my solution?
- How do I deliver that solution?
- How big is my company?
- Do I have a team? If so, how many people does it consist of and who are they?
- What is my revenue and profit?
- How much do I earn personally?
- What is the role of technology in my company?
- In which area do I enable innovation?
- Who knows me? Only my clients? Or am I more widely visible?

One of my goals, for example, is by 2030, 70% of all entrepreneurs in the Netherlands will know the Profit First method.

Strategy

If your mission and vision are clear, and you know what you have to do to make your vision come true, it is important that you think about the way in which you can achieve your goals. What is the path you are going to follow?

The word "strategy" may seem vague and theoretical. You're already seeing yourself writing and sweating for days, and by the time your strategic plan is finished, it'll be outdated, and you'll stash it in a drawer. I agree with you; that would be a real waste of your time and energy. So, let's not do that.

However, I do advise you to think about how you are going to achieve your goals. If you want more sales, are you going to increase your prices or double your client base? If you want to grow from a hundred to a thousand clients in three years, what is your plan? Are you going to take over another company? Do you make sure that every client brings in a new lead? Are you going to give keynotes to increase visibility? Will you give away an e-book in exchange for email addresses through Facebook ads?

And talking about new clients: are all those new clients going to buy your current product or do you want them to buy something else from you? You need to know how you are going to reach your goal, otherwise you will have no idea what to do next week, tomorrow, today.

From outline to details

Nobody knows today what the world will look like next year. Therefore, don't bother trying to work out in detail how you will achieve your goals next year. It is essential that you have a general idea of how you will achieve your goals. This can be summarized on one sheet of paper or even in one paragraph.

For example:

Goal:

By 2030, 70% of all entrepreneurs will know the Profit First method.

Strategy:

1. Training, certifying, and supporting of X number of Profit First Professionals each year.

2. Giving ten lectures per year to groups of at least 150 entrepreneurs.

3. Publish an article or do a media interview about The Profit Advisor or Profit First six times a year.

Once the outline has been established, don't look ahead for more than a quarter or a maximum of one year.

Schedule time and ask for help

You don't determine your strategy in one random hour crammed into a busy Monday in September. Preferably, you will schedule several half days for this, during which you and your team, away from your workplace, will only discuss one subject: how are we going to achieve our goals? If you don't know how to do this yourself, hire a business coach or Profit First Professional, who will guide you through the steps in a methodical way.

From long-term goals via strategy to daily actions

Your mission can be life-changing, your vision magical, your strategy as neat as a pin, but if you don't do the right things today, nothing will happen. Ultimately, success depends on one thing only: doing the right things consistently.

The big question is how to move from your mission, vision, strategy and long-term goals to concrete actions that you can perform in the present. You do this by gradually translating your long-term goals to actions that you can carry out today.

Every day anew you have to know what that one thing is that you have to do. You can only know that if you have a clear vision of how today's actions will lead you to achieving your vision.

You formulate your goals from abstract to concrete and from big to small. To know what to do today, you need to know what your goal for this week is. To know what your goal for this week is, you need to know what your goal is for this month, this quarter, and this year. To know what you must focus on this year, you need to know what your goal is for five years from now.

Goal for the coming year

Once you've determined where you want to be in five, ten, or fifteen years' time, you can formulate what you want to achieve this year. It is important that your goal should be profitable, achievable, and ambitious. A goal that does not lead to profit is not a sustainable goal. A goal that is not feasible demotivates. A goal that is not ambitious demotivates because of its dullness.

For example:

Goals for this year:

1. Train, certify, and support 100 Profit First Professionals.

2. Speak once for a group of at least 1,000 entrepreneurs and three times for groups of at least 150 entrepreneurs.

3. Be interviewed on national TV about The Profit Advisor.

Do you work with a team? Then make sure the goal is supported by your team, so your team members can align their daily actions with your goal. My team knows that training, certifying, and supporting Profit First Professionals is my main goal this year.

As soon as my staff faces time constraints or any other obstacle, they will know that work related to Profit First Professionals is always more important than other tasks. This gives clarity, it helps make the right choices and it saves me a lot of time and energy because things I have delegated to my team do not come back to me via a detour.

Goal for this quarter

A year lasts a long time, so an annual goal – important as it may be – will soon be set aside. After all, you still have a year ;-) Based on your goal for the year you and your team establish quarterly goals at the start of each quarter. Quarterly goals are not just 'nice to haves.' The intention is that they will be achieved this quarter. That creates success experiences: you and your team are working on making your vision come true and that is a strong motivator. As soon as quarterly goals do not get achieved, you and your team will get bogged down again in the issues of the day. That is not the end of the world, but make sure that you schedule and refocus on your goals the following quarter.

Quarterly goals should be assigned to a person. One person should be responsible for achieving each goal to ensure accountability. Make sure each and every quarterly goal is achievable. Three to seven goals per person per quarter are generally easy to achieve. This, of course, depends on the type of goal. Quarterly goals are not a to-do list from which you can pick things as you like. These are all goals that contribute to the bigger picture and, therefore, really must all be achieved.

Make sure your goals are visible. Write them on a whiteboard, hang them on a cupboard in the office pantry and mention them every week at the start of the team meeting. Make sure everyone is on board and knows what the focus is each quarter.

Goal for this month, this week, today

Based on the quarterly goals, team members determine their own monthly and weekly goals. From the weekly objectives, team members determine daily goals at the beginning of each workday.

I use a very practical solution for myself. I divided a large flip-over sheet into nine quadrants, as in Figure 6.

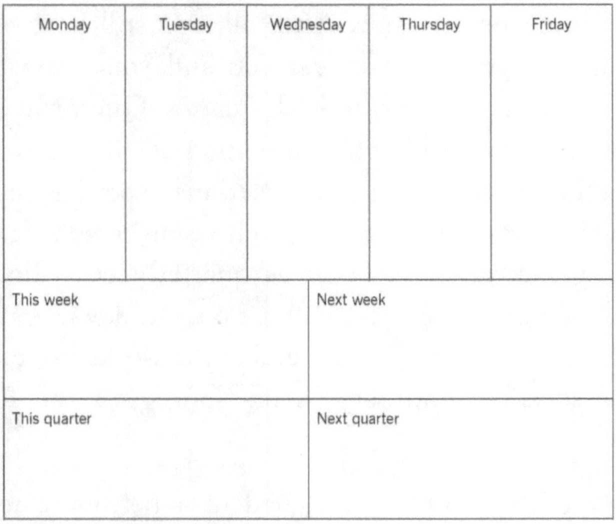

Monday	Tuesday	Wednesday	Thursday	Friday
This week			Next week	
This quarter			Next quarter	

Figure 6: *Scheduling example*

From left to right are the days of the week. Below that are the boxes for this week, next week, this quarter, and next quarter. I work with post-its on which I've written my goals. Every Monday morning, I determine the most important goals for this week, based on my quarterly goals.

At this stage I give myself room to add to-do items to my weekly plan. This gives me a good insight into what I need to do every day. It helps me make choices: what will I do and what not? Moreover, I have a strong focus, because I know exactly what to do today to achieve my goals this month, this quarter, and this year. Being successful is, therefore, not a matter of luck or coincidence, but something I consciously work on every day.

11.3 Processes

Now that you know why you do what you do, where you want to go, and how you are going to achieve that goal, it is important to design your business processes in such a way that you will achieve your goals in the most efficient way, while still ensuring excellent quality.

In his bestseller: *The E-Myth Revisited: Why Most Small Businesses Don't Work and What to Do About It*, Michael E. Gerber challenges you to set up your company as if you wanted to franchise it. He cites McDonald's as a shining example: wherever you buy your burger in the world, you get the same service, the same speed, the same smile, and more or less the same product. And McDonald's also makes money doing that. The group's success does not depend on whether the McDonald's CEO gets out of bed in the morning bright-eyed and bushy-tailed or with a runny nose. McDonald's is successful because it offers an identical solution to their clients' demands in the most efficient way and according to fixed processes. It's up to you, Gerber says, to set up your business as if you were going to franchise it. Make sure you have a standard solution for your client's problem and avoid making that solution dependent on you or specific team members. Solutions that depend on specific people limit your ability to scale your process and your company.

I found it an intriguing question: how would I set up my business as if I wanted to franchise it? What are my clients' main problems/questions and which standard should I apply to ensure that my processes will produce a high-quality solution every time, and as efficiently as possible?

If you have a bookkeeping or accounting firm, several of your client's issues are clear: the accounts must be in order, the sales tax returns must be taken care of, and the income tax or corporate tax returns must be filed. There are at least three problems that most small accounting firms experience in solving problems:

1. Dependence on the skills and qualities of people.

2. Ascribing too much value to your own knowledge and skills.

3. Letting the client direct the work.

1. Dependence on the skills and qualities of people

I see that in many companies, each employee determines how the client is being helped. Each employee has her own vision, working method, and preferences, but also her own qualities and shortcomings. One employee is very structured and another claims to be able to retrieve anything from the piled up mess covering his desk. One delivers top performance under high pressure, whereas another can only cope with one activity at a time. One has made delivery lists for his clients, which another looks at with amazement. "Hey," you see him think, "that's handy, I'd like to have one of those too!" It takes one four times longer to do the same job than another. In short, there's no single process or system in place.

Now you may think that makes sense. Different employees have different characters, strengths and weaknesses, qualities, pitfalls and skills. Of course, part of the success of your company is due to hiring the right employees. But you will undoubtedly also recognize that the wheel gets reinvented over and over again. That you are sometimes surprised by the inefficiency in certain tasks and that you have often thought spending time on developing the right format could save a lot of time in the long run. But still you don't have enough standard procedures in your company. The daily pressure, the continuous flow of questions, actions, and tasks is so great that there is simply no time left to put the foundations in order. And by continuing to accept that you are so busy with work in your company that there is never time to work on your company, you remain trapped in a vicious circle. You remain an employee in your own company instead of becoming the CEO of your company.

2. *Ascribing too much value to your own knowledge and skills*

In addition to the dependence on the knowledge and skills of employees, there is another major obstacle that experts have to overcome before they become leaders: attaching too much value to their own abilities. I hear, "In the time it takes me to explain it, I can do it myself five times." Or, "No one can do this as well as I can." All experts say that. I have said it myself for years too. And, of course, it's often true. Chances are that this was one of the reasons why you started your own company. You discovered that you did things better and faster than others. In fact, that is what clients and your boss told you.

But as long as you use your qualities as a financial expert as a criterion to run your company, you will never be able to step off the treadmill. If you really want to do everything yourself, accept that you have a job. And accept that you are your company and that your company cannot function separately from you.

3. *Letting the client dictate the work*

The third problem I want to mention concerns the client. In many accounting firms, the client dictates what happens on each particular day. Does the client submit receipts? Then they are processed that day or sometime that week. Does the client need a financial statement for a financing application? Then all other work is pushed aside for this "emergency". After all, the client always comes first. But a company in which most of the work is scheduled by the client cannot be run efficiently.

The client creates chaos that you clean up. No wonder we have a thousand and one things on our hands, and we are forever lagging behind. No wonder we feel we are not in control. Because we are not in control. "Can it be any other way then?" you ask yourself? Yes, there certainly is another way. And the great thing is that it not only benefits you, but also – or perhaps especially – the client.

One of your clients' main problems is that bookkeeping always comes last. They don't want to do it; there are always more urgent matters. They must call clients, write newsletters. The bookkeeping can always be done tomorrow. But if your clients say that every week and every month, they will face the consequences. They will accumulate huge accounting backlogs, will have to search everywhere for receipts and invoices, will have no idea where to start, and will have to work well into the night. The aversion to accounting is growing stronger. And yet they've never experienced the benefits of accounting – understanding their financial data as a basis for decision-making. As soon as you inform the client about how things are done within your company, what you need when, and what they get in return, you help them to implement accounting habits. The benefits are enormous. They create peace and gain insight. They sleep again at night and sometimes even feel like looking at their figures. They will be eternally grateful for these changes, and they'll be willing to pay a premium to their profit advisor.

The most important problems in the transformation from having a job to running a company are summarized below:

- It is people, employees and business owner who are

responsible for the quality and speed of the work delivered.
- The owner can do everything faster and better than others and sees that as a criterion for who does what.
- The client dictates what happens when, which results in chaos.

Describing processes

The solution to the problems described above is to set up your company as if you wanted to set up a franchise. This means you think about what the most important results or products are, which steps need to be taken to achieve them, and then you describe those steps. The whole of the results, processes, and system is preferably unique to your company, which will ultimately distinguish you from the competition.

The following example will clarify this principle. Filing the tax return is an example of a process that is executed over and over again, but probably with varying results. Maggie's clients always submit everything in full, whereas Martin constantly must chase after missing documents. Daniel files the tax return for 80 of his clients before the summer, whereas Carmen does not file any tax returns for her clients before the summer. William files more returns than any of the others.

Let's use this example to go through the steps of describing a process.

Step 1 – Identify the most important products/results

What is the result of the process? A good answer to this question can only be given if you have total clarity about your mission, vision and strategy, goals and the interdependence of the processes. In the example of filing the tax return, the desired result can be filing the return on or before the date agreed with the client.

Step 2 – Design the steps to be taken to achieve that result

This step is not so much about the steps taken to achieve the result in the current situation, but about the steps that need to be taken to achieve the expressed result within your vision, mission, and strategy as effectively and efficiently as possible. Our example would cover the exact steps that must be followed to file a tax return.

Step 3 – Describe the steps

The third step describes the process or records it on video or audio so that anyone can read, watch or listen to it.

There are some common bottlenecks in this step:

1. *This step is skipped.* The often-heard excuse is that it takes too much time and/or by the time the process is written out, it is already outdated. Holding on to this excuse means that your company will remain dependent on your presence and your decisions. It means that you will never really get where you want to be. This step is essential, but don't make it any bigger than necessary. A process description does not need to be ten pages long. Perhaps it is not even necessary to commit a process description to paper at all. For example, if you want to describe a process that takes place on a computer, take a screen recording while you're performing it. The necessary software costs about $100 dollars, a one-time expense. But even a description on paper sometimes only needs to be one page long. Since the process is usually already in your head, it can be transferred to paper in 20 minutes. And after that, you can share or delegate the process.

2. *This step is carried out in too much detail.* Describing a

process does not have to take a full day. It helps to bear in mind that it will never be perfect. As soon as something is on paper, it can be put into use. Any adjustments can be made while working with the process.

3. *Too little information is given.* The opposite also happens quite a lot. A description is so compact that another person has no idea what to do with it. The "process owner," an expert, forgets that another person must start at the very beginning. It helps to include at least the following parts in the process description:

– *Goal of this process*: what is the final product of this process?

– *Process steps*: what steps does this process contain?

– *Per-process step*: who does it, when should it be done, and possibly an explanation.

The process in our example then looks like Figure 7.

Process: tax return				
Process goal: Filing the tax return on or before the date agreed with the client				
No.	Step	Who	When	Explanation
1	Discuss filing date and timelines with client	Accountant	January	• Add submission date to team calendar • Confirm timelines in writing to client and add to project planning
2	Send submission list	Secretary	First week of February	• Submission list: Dropbox/standard emails/income tax submission list
3	Check that documents have been received on time	Secretary	From March	• All clients' submission dates are included in the project planning • In case of missing documents request client to complete submission; if complete: inform bookkeeper that client information is complete
4	Save documents	Secretary	Upon receipt	• Save documents in client specific folder
...	Et cetera			

Figure 7: *Example of a process description*

Step 4 – Train your team to perform the process

In step 4, the team has been trained to perform the process, so that everyone knows what is expected. Because professionals are often averse to bureaucracy, this step requires leadership from you. It is essential that team members understand the benefits for themselves. It is very likely that they will find it helpful, for example, to have a list of questions that must be asked during every intake interview. It would be a good thing to start with a process whose benefits are obvious to the team members. As soon as they experience the benefits of having and following a fixed process, any resistance will vanish. The example process outlined earlier shows, for example, that the secretary can take over a lot of the work. There is a good chance that this process will be welcomed with open arms.

Step 5 – Improve the process

A company is not a static entity, and neither is a process. Goals change, strategies change, insights change, and processes evolve as well. Every time you or someone in your team feels that a process can be better, faster, or cheaper, the process description must be adjusted. If that does not happen, a process description soon becomes outdated.

Improving a process description in a beautifully printed hardcover company handbook is impossible. Make sure your process descriptions are on a shared drive in the cloud, so everyone can access them. Also, don't introduce unnecessary bureaucratic actions, such as wanting to approve every adjustment to a process.

Once a process has been handed over to team members, it becomes their process, and you don't have to worry about it anymore. When things start going to go wrong and goals are not being accomplished, you know it is time to interfere, but not sooner.

How to start?

Describing all business processes can seem like an impossible task – and it probably is. In my view, it's also unnecessary. The idea is to save a lot of time and money and achieve better results by mapping and describing the most important processes. Therefore, start with the most important process, the process that you know can be profitable in all respects.

The following processes probably deserve attention. Each process includes a list of questions you ask.

Processing the client administration

- How and when do I want clients to submit documents?
- How often and in what way do we process the client's administration?
- How do we communicate questions regarding the documents submitted?
- How do we deal with clients who fail to submit their administration correctly/on time/in full?
- Which standard e-mails and letters do we use in this process? Where and how do we store them?

Reporting to the client

- Which standard reports do we provide?
- Which reports do we provide on request?
- How often do we report?
- How do we report?
- How do we deal with client queries regarding the reports?

- How and where do we store the client's reports?
- Which standard e-mails and letters do we use in this process? Where and how do we store them?

Filing the tax return

- What are the standard steps we follow to file the tax return? You assume that all the documents have been processed, because the "processing client administration" process runs smoothly.
- When and how do we communicate with the client within this process?
- Which standard e-mails and letters do we use in this process? Where and how do we store them?
- What are common exceptions and how do we treat them?

11.4 Systems and automation

You should not do yourself what a computer can do for you. This very simple rule is the key message of this section. A computer does the job cheaper, faster and with fewer errors. However, optimizing the use of systems is not that simple. It all starts with the following question: "Which system from the dozens of systems available will we use?" Then the system must be implemented, linked to other systems, and the team must learn to work with it.

Moreover, the changes in the process that this new system entails must be implemented and perhaps also communicated to the client. We often feel like there's simply no time for all that. So, you keep doing what you have always done, and you keep losing time and money every day.

If you want to take the next step in your company, you will

simply have to structurally make time and money available to deepen your knowledge of systems. This is not a one-off action. Technological developments are happening so fast that you too must continuously keep innovating.

Choosing a system

As soon as there are several systems for one desired result, you must make a choice. This applies, for example, to the accounting system you are going to work with, but also to the server, the backup system, the calendar, the phones, the declaration software and the webinar software, among others.

To choose the right system from the many dozens or sometimes hundreds of systems, you must know exactly what that system has to do for you. You need an overview of the specifications. The better you and your team know what the system should do for you, the easier it is to choose the right system. Include the below considerations in your specifications:

- What is the required output?
- Distinguish between users: team, client, others.
- What reports should the system generate?
- What links with other systems are needed?
- Does the system run locally or online? (Software as a Service: SaaS)
- Are there specific security and backup requirements?
- Do different user profiles have to be created?
- How many users should be able to work with the system simultaneously?
- What is the budget?

On the basis of the specs, you will talk to experts, suppliers and partners to find the right system. I will briefly explain several systems that facilitate the work of a profit adviser.

Accounting software

Choosing accounting software is probably one of the most important choices for a bookkeeping or accounting firm. Many accounting firms work with the client's preferred software but that causes quite a few problems. Once you work with multiple systems, your team must be trained in all these different systems, all other systems must be linked to those systems, all processes must connect to those systems and so forth. You should understand that this is not the most efficient way of working. Choosing a single system for everyone in the company saves a lot of time and money. You may lose potential clients because of this, but at the same time you will create room for clients who do want to work with your preferred system, and who will therefore generate much more profit for you. Moreover, they are easier to find, because you have a clear marketing message.

Meeting software

Meeting face-to-face provides added value over and above calling each other or meeting online. But always meeting face-to-face takes too much time in relation to what it yields. There are some conversations you want to have while sitting at the same table, such as the intake interview. And especially when I work together with a client on his plans for half a day, I prefer to do so face-to-face.

Many other meetings can just as easily take place via online meeting tools. Driving to your clients will add hours to your timesheet, and the same goes for clients who come to you, taking valuable time they could be spending on growing their business.

Tools like Skype or Zoom give you the opportunity to give your clients a personal touch while saving time. Zoom and other online meeting tools have free versions, but there are also more advanced, paid tools.

Online appointment calendar

Just making an appointment doesn't seem like a big deal, but often a lot of time is wasted emailing back and forth to arrive at a mutually agreeable time. And we all know scheduling changes crop up all the time. An online calendar that synchronizes with your own calendar takes a lot of work off your hands. Your clients book appointments themselves, and they automatically appear in your online calendar. There are several free or paid online calendars available. Calendly and Acuity are widely used.

Social media management tools

If you use social media for business purposes, you will soon discover that posting regular updates there takes a lot of time. But regular updates are one of the keys factors in achieving success on social media. That is where social media management tools come in handy. You save a lot of time by scheduling all tips, updates, and blogs for a week or even a month in one go. Of course, you can spontaneously post things in between, but at least you have a foundation that you no longer need to look at. Much used social media management tools are Buffer, Hootsuite and Post Planner.

Project planner

Once you work with a team, there are tasks that need to be handed over. This can be done by email or through meetings, but neither option is very efficient. An online planning tool is a perfect way to organize all tasks and projects. I have been working with the free version of Teamwork for years, but Trello and Asana are also widely used systems.

Online learning environment

As part of your program, you transfer knowledge and skills to clients. Not surprisingly, it's not efficient to do that in person, because every time you do, it takes time. Moreover, after a while it gets boring to have to tell the same story again. It is a lot more efficient to develop the contents of the program properly once – in a video, audio, or e-book – and to refer to it every time. Once teaching becomes a significant part of your services and products, consider developing an online learning environment. New clients are given access to it, so they can access the material easily and from any location.

11.5 Building and maintaining a strong team

You have automated everything that can be automated. The processes are designed in such a way that the results do not depend on you or a specific team member's knowledge and skills: these are important steps. But it's not yet the complete answer to the question of how to turn your company into a driven organization that solves the client's problem in the most efficient way. In almost all cases, you need people to carry out parts of the process... your team.

Building and maintaining a good team that propagates the company vision, does what needs to be done, delivers value and fits within the organization is not always easy. There are two aspects in building a team that often go wrong:

- *Tasks and responsibilities are divided ambiguously.*

If there is more work than the current team can handle, you hire new staff. That person is often intended to fill in the existing gaps. When a company hires several employees in this way, tasks and responsibilities become mixed up and intertwined. The management assistant also happens to do the Facebook ads. One of the first bookkeepers on the team takes care of invoicing. The owner does credit management, because she's always done it, and nobody asked who would be a more suitable person for that task. Because new clients turn up regularly, no one is specifically responsible for acquisition. If there are no new clients for a while, no one knows how to do acquisition and which team member is responsible for it. Nightmare scenarios like this one play out in companies all over the world, but it's a situation we can avoid.

- *"Hitting it off" is not a reproducible criterion.*

New team members are hired when they have the required diplomas and skills, and when you "hit it off." But it is impossible to say why you hit it off or not, so it is not possible to reproduce a great match or avoid a complete disaster.

In *Get a Grip*, Gino Wickman presents two solutions to tackling the above problems:

1. Seats before people

Wickman recommends that functions – seats – be separated from people. Most of the time, though, that's not what we do. In practice, you have great people who are in the wrong job and team members who are perfect on paper, but who just don't fit within the company:

- *Right person, wrong seat* – This person is a perfect match within the organization. He shares the company's values, hits it off with the team, but still doesn't function fully because he's in the wrong seat. He tries to do things he can't or won't do well.
- *Right seat, wrong person* – This person has the right role and function on paper but doesn't fit the company or contribute to the vision, mission and goals of the organization. Nobody can really put their finger on it,

but everyone feels that things are not right. This problem often also applies to existing staff. People do not get on, but nobody can explain why. Instead of taking action, we just let the situation fester.

According to Wickman, when forming and retaining your team, you must first look at which seats in your company should be filled before you look at who should be sitting on those seats. This gives you, especially if you have an existing team that is not functioning properly, all the room you need to make decisions without being obscured by emotions. Are you about to expand your team? Then dare to let go of the people you currently employ. First of all, ask yourself which seats need to be filled. In other words: draw an organigram. It's quite difficult to do without thinking about specific people. You may be tempted to say, "No, we don't have a budget to hire someone for marketing." Or, "Pascal already does human resources, doesn't he?" Given the fact that Pascal was originally hired as a financial controller, you need to free yourself from the constraints of your current staff arrangement. Always tell yourself, "We'll look at people later. First, let's see which seats we have."

An example of an organigram of a small SME can be seen in Figure 8.

Figure 8: *Example of an organigram of a small business*

Once the seats have been determined, you need to determine, for each seat, which four or five responsibilities belong to that seat. These are not job descriptions of multiple pages, but just several bullet points. For example:

CEO:

– Protect the vision and mission

– Develop and monitor the strategy

– Manage the management team

Finance:

– Manage the finance team

– Control the budget

– et cetera

Marketing & Sales:

– Manage the M&S team

– Achieve M&S goals

– et cetera

2. *Attracting the right people*

As soon as you and your management team agree on the seats to be filled, it is important to go and look for the right people for those seats. If you have a small business, it may well be that one person will initially occupy several seats. But it is then completely clear who is responsible when something is not going according to plan.

The big question is how to attract the right people. Just looking at knowledge and skills is usually not enough. You are looking for much more in a team member than just knowledge and skills. Hitting it off is not a sufficient reason either, especially as you are not always sure how to determine which candidates are an ideal fit.

According to Wickman, you should look for people who share your vision and mission and who also match the core values that are important to your company. The most important core values of your company are determined in four steps:

1. Establish which people from your current team fit best within the team.

2. For each team member, make a list of his or her characteristics and values.

3. Put the lists next to each other: which characteristics and values are shared by several team members?

4. Reduce the total list to approximately five most important core values for your company.

When you attract new team members, you check your vision and mission with them. It is essential that your vision and mission make candidates super enthusiastic and are in line with their own vision and mission. Then judge the potential team member based on your company's core values. Candidates who don't score positively on all the core values aren't the right match.

If some of your existing team members aren't functioning well, compare them to your core values and discuss your findings. If they see an opportunity to improve on the concerning core value, you have created a stronger team. If that doesn't work, then it's no surprise that you will have to let them go.

Action step

Schedule a "team away-day" to reflect on your goals, strategy, and plan. Also determine what the most important processes are within the company and start by describing those processes.

Take a close look at the systems. Which systems need to be replaced? Which systems that you need are not yet in place? Determine which seats you have within the company, which responsibilities belong to each seat, and which core values apply within your company, so that you can see how both current and new personnel score on these core values.

In this last chapter of *The Profit Advisor* I gave you tools to build a company that is not entirely dependent on you. You want your company to be able to deliver the solution, even when you are not at work yourself. I would like to remind you once again of my definition of a company: *a driven, profitable organization which sells a solution to solve the client's problem and delivers this solution as efficiently as possible.*

This definition contains nine essential elements that have all been addressed in this book. In this last chapter, you looked at your own organization and the ways to deliver the solution as efficiently as possible. Building an organization that also delivers value when you're not at work is perhaps the icing on the cake.

I wrote this book in three-and-a-half months. That may seem like a short time for writing a book, but I stopped doing many things during that time. For example, I stopped selling my program. And yet I paid my team and suppliers all these months, received my salary and even made a profit. That was not thanks to luck or winning a lottery. I have built a company that is not entirely dependent on me. What will you do with the room you create when your company no longer needs you all the time to deliver value and earn money?

CONCLUSION AND IMPLEMENTATION PLAN

I've given you everything. I included in this book all the knowledge, methods, skills, and techniques I have used in working with my clients over the past ten years. Now it is up to you. It is up to you to give this information a place, to make it your own and to use it in a way that suits you the best and creates the most value to your clients.

Dozens of bookkeepers and accountants read this book before its publication. They told me there was a lot of information in it. Some even said there was too much ;-) Do you need help with the implementation of the information in this book in your company?

Do not hesitate to contact me via ProfitFirstProfessionals.nl or femke@profitfirst.nl.

Do you want to get started by yourself first? Then I'd be happy to give you an implementation plan. You can download it for free from www.theprofitadvisor.eu.

BIBLIOGRAPHY

Laura Babeliowsky (2015), *Het geheim van 100.000 per jaar. Heel goed verdienen met het werk dat je het liefste doet.* Culemborg: Van Duuren Management.

Michael E. Gerber (1995), *The E-Myth revisited. Why most small businesses don't work and what to do about it.* New York: HarperCollins Publishers.

Femke Hogema (2018), *Financiën voor zzp'ers en andere zelfstandige ondernemers. Hoe je een financieel gezond bedrijf runt. (Finance for solopreneurs)* Culemborg: Van Duuren Management.

Femke Hogema (2019), *Winstgevende Plannen. In 7 stappen een financieel succesvol bedrijf. (Profitable Plans)* Culemburg: Van Duuren Management.

Gary Keller (2013), *The ONE Thing: The Surprisingly Simple Truth Behind Extraordinary Results.* Austin, TX: Bard Press.

Mike Michalowicz (2012), *The Pumpkin Plan. A simple strategy to grow a remarkable business in any field*. New York: Penguin Group.

Mike Michalowicz (2017), *Profit First: Transform Your Business from a Cash-Eating Monster to a Money-Making Machine*. New York: Portfolio Penguin.

Mike Michalowicz (2018), *Clockwork. Design Your Business to Run Itself*. New York: Penguin Group.

Tony Robbins (2001), *Awake the Giant within. Take immediate control of your mental, emotional, physical and financial destiny*. London: Simon and Schuster.

Simon Sinek (2009), *Start with why. How great leaders inspire everyone to take action*. London: Penguin Group.

Gino Wickman & Mike Paton (2014), *Get a Grip. How to get everything you want from your entrepreneurial business*. Dallas: BenBella Books, Inc.

ABOUT THE AUTHOR

Femke Hogema started her career as a financial controller for large international companies. She loved figures and the clarity that figures provide about a company's health. But she also saw that entrepreneurs don't like figures, controllers, bookkeepers, or accountants. Entrepreneurs find figures boring, complicated, and theoretical. She started her company, Healthy Finance, to close this gap between entrepreneurs and figures, and to help entrepreneurs get a grip on their numbers. She gave lectures and training courses, wrote the bestseller *Financiën voor zzp'ers* (*Finance for solopreneurs*) and contributed to the Dutch edition of *Profit First*. Femke makes figures fun, practical, and accessible and in the course of ten years she inspired tens of thousands of entrepreneurs to build a financially healthy and profitable business.

Since 2017, Femke has focused on training accountants and bookkeepers to become Profit Advisors (through Profit First Professionals Netherlands). She teaches accountants and bookkeepers so that they can, in turn, support entrepreneurs in growing a financially healthy and profitable business. Femke loves to teach clients to build their own profitable company which will yield more pleasure and satisfaction.

Femke was featured as financial coach in a popular TV show on National TV. In 2019 she wrote a number one bestseller *Winstgevende Plannen* (*Profitable Plans*). The book reached a number one position in the Dutch National Management Book Top 100 within one and a half week after publication and kept that position for 28 days.

She gives keynotes in both the Dutch and English language about The Profit Advisor, Profit First and Profitable Plans.

ACKNOWLEDGMENTS

Publishing a book is a big deal. And publishing an international book is something that seemed to be completely out of my league, until it happened.

I am grateful to be surrounded by people who believed in me and therefore helped me believe in myself.

First of all, thank you Ina Boer, Van Duuren Management, for your confidence in me and this book. You did not hesitate a second to publish this book in The Netherlands and I am very grateful for that.

Thank you Liesbeth Heenk, Amsterdam Publishers, for your confidence to publish this book internationally.

Thank you Ron Rosenbrand, Betterwords, for the initial translation to English and Meggan Robinson for the excellent proofread. You totally got my style!

Thank you Dr. Sabrina Starling, Benita Königbauer, Cyndi Thomason, Lisa Campbell, Damon Yudichak and Maja Donker for the feedback on the English edition.

Thank you Mike Michalowicz, Ron Saharyan and all the other peeps at Profit First Professionals HQ, Sonja Akkies-Grilk, Maja Donker and the rest of the team at Profit First Professionals BV and all the Profit First Professionals all over the world for your knowledge and inspiration.

Last but not least, thank you Bart Schat, Daan and Rein. For being the most important people in my world.

www.ingramcontent.com/pod-product-compliance
Lightning Source LLC
LaVergne TN
LVHW091632070526
838199LV00044B/1040